W9-BUM-806

SIMÓN BOLÍVAR: EDUCATOR

BY LUIS B. PRIETO

TRANSLATED BY JAMES D. PARSONS

1970/GARDEN CITY, NEW YORK

Simón Bolívar:
Educator

DOUBLEDAY & COMPANY, INC.

Library of Congress Catalog Card Number 73–97676
Copyright © 1970 by Doubleday & Company, Inc.
All Rights Reserved
Printed in the United States of America
First Edition

PREFACE

This essay is the product of a long process of study and research. In Problemas de la educación venezolana,[1] *I touched on the Bolivarian theme of the Commission on Education and commented on some of its activities in relation to the "professional estate." In various essays and articles I have referred to the preoccupation of the Liberator with the problems of education.*

In Havana during the years 1950 and 1951, I gave a series of lectures on Bolívar's ideas about education as part of a course in comparative education directed by Dr. Emma Pérez Tellez, whom I served as ad honorem *assistant, and, in the program on adult education in Latin America, as part of a course I gave in the summer school of Havana University, I included the discussion of some problems concerning the functioning of the Moral Power—a fourth branch of government proposed by Bolívar that is of fundamental concern in his design for public education. In that same city, where I had sufficient free time but not the necessary serenity of spirit, I began to document my studies from the books of various authors (Diderot, Rousseau, Helvetius, and other writers in French, as well as writers in other languages) that were present in the National Library of Cuba, situated in the old Castle of the Prince. I was spurred on by the aim of condensing into a well-documented book whatever is known about Bolívar's attitudes toward education and about his extensive thoughts on the education of the people. Toward this end, I gathered notes in two thick notebooks, but they were unfortunately lost in my travels from one country to another, where I carried out my activities as educator in exile, in the service of UNESCO.*

In Tegucigalpa in 1957, I gave a lecture at Francisco Morazán Normal School, named after the early-nineteenth-century champion of popular education and of Central American federation, a lecture that had the same title as the present work in its Spanish edition: El magisterio americano de Bolívar. *Stenographic notes from that lecture have served as a guide in the writing of the essay now placed before the reader.*

*I have sometimes thought I would never have time to com-
plete this book, and for this reason proposed that the material
which is the object of my concern be adopted as the thesis of a
doctoral dissertation in the Seminar on the Problems of Education in Venezuela that I was directing in the School of Humanities and Education at our Central University. As was customary,
in accordance with the technical requirements of the work in a
seminar, I outlined the theme and drew up the bibliography and
a list of possible research sources for the student involved, but
the dissertation never came into being. Eight years have passed
since then, and during that time, by robbing hours away from
rest and spending nights without sleep, I have brought to com-
pletion the work I began more than twenty years ago.*

*In this task I have received invaluable help that I wish to
point out here in order to express my gratitude: first of all to
the National Library of France, from whom I received microfilm
copies of various books that are out of print and unobtainable
(such as the* Essai d'éducation nationale *of La Chalotais,* Rapport
et Projet de Décret sur l'organisation generale de l'instruction
publique *of Condorcet,* Essai sur l'histoire et sur l'état actuel de
l'instruction publique en France *of Guizot,* L'Instruction publique en France pendant la Revolution, Debats legislatifs, *all of
them cited in the text of this work), to Dr. Juan Oropesa, who
procured these copies from the library, to Professor Daniel
Navea Acevedo, who died at the fall of the Salto de La Llovizna
Bridge in Caroní on August 23, 1964. In his baggage Professor
Navea was carrying a copy of the first draft of this work, duly
annotated in order for us to discuss it during the time that we
were to have free at the Venezuelan Conference on Education,
which met there. Let this memorial stand as a token of his loyal
friendship and of my sincere affection. I would also like to express my gratitude to José Nucete Sardi, to Dr. Ramón J.
Velásquez, and to Professor Elena Martínez Chacón, all of whom
read copies of that first draft and offered valuable suggestions;
to Drs. Luis Villalba Villalba, Pedro Grases, Rafael Armando
Rojas, J. L. Salcedo Bastardo, Guillermo Morón, José Lorenzo
Pérez, Evangelina García, Pablo Ojer, S.J., to Professor Pedro
Díaz Seijas and Manuel Pérez Vila, who attended the collective
reading of the book and made many perceptive observations;
to the National Library of Venezuela, for the co-operation given*

*me by offering important works for consultation from their moun-
tain of books; to the artist Mateo Manaure, who took care of the
illustrations and designed the cover for the Spanish edition; to
my secretary, Alicia de González, who has copied, corrected,
and copied again and again all the successive versions of this
work; and finally, to Adolfo Olivo Armand, who did the analytical indexes and who saw the book through the press in its
original Spanish edition.*

LUIS B. PRIETO FIGUEROA

CARACAS, MAY 1968

PROLOGUE

This work has two main purposes: to call attention to the qualities that characterized Simón Bolívar as a great instructor in the
exercise of freedom, and to find the roots, both near and far, of
possible influences on his ideas about education. This latter task,
while subordinate to the first, is nevertheless an essential part
of the work, since unfounded statements have been made of
such a nature that I am required to try to disprove them or at
least to indicate what their true limits are.

It has become practically a commonplace to say that Bolívar's
ideas, especially his social and political ideas, are derived from
Jean Jacques Rousseau, either directly or by way of his teacher,
Simón Rodríguez.

Gil Fortoul in the first volume of his extraordinary *Historia
constitutional de Venezuela,* published in 1907, indicated the
influence on the student Bolívar of the teacher Rodríguez, with
whom, "talking and traveling, he began to acquire that vast
knowledge of political and literary matters that he disclosed later
in his letters, speeches, proclamations, and constitutional proposals; under his direction, he became familiar with the works
of the English philosophers, with the French Encyclopedists, and
with ancient and modern classics, historians, philosophers, orators, poets; with him, he carefully read Montesquieu and Rousseau, whose theories and even whose style served him many
times as a model." Gil Fortoul insists on the overwhelming influence of Rousseau on Bolívar. He says that the works of the
latter "above all imitated certain peculiarities of style" of the
former.[2]

Jules Mancini in his biography of Bolívar amplifies these notions of Gil Fortoul,[3] even while he acknowledges as "true that
the powerful personality of the Liberator is not one in which
it is easy to find foreign influences. But it is not possible," continues Mancini, "for him to remove himself from the ascendancy
of the men whose thought and whose actions dominated the
century, and it is from Jean Jacques and from Napoleon that
Bolívar is to seek lessons and examples . . . To them he owes,

if we might express ourselves in this way, his accomplished glories and his accomplished errors." Mancini goes so far as to say that "he takes from the *Discourses* the basic terms of his vocabulary, to such a degree that, reading Bolívar, one believes oneself at times to be reading a translation of Rousseau."[4] Gil Fortoul had said that "the language of Bolívar, then and always, was plagued with Gallicisms, to such a degree that reading him one cannot help thinking that he thought in French in order to write in Spanish."[5]

These statements by Gil Fortoul and by Mancini, which have contributed to the disorientation of many people, appear to have been proven false by a specialist who has a great reputation for diligence and wide learning in linguistics, Professor Angel Rosenblatt. In his Introduction to the book *La lengua de Bolívar,* by Martha Hildebrandt, he argues, "The spiritual heritage of the Liberator—and his language is the blood of his spirit—is profoundly Hispanic. Bolívar is a great writer in the Spanish language, who can be compared linguistically with the priest Feijoo or with Jovellanos. From his most intimate letters to his speeches and military proclamations, he is the master of all the expressive resources of his language and he handles it as a personal endowment." However, Rosenblatt does acknowledge, after due reflection, that, "like the whole Spanish world of his time, he was open above all to French influence."[6]

Dr. Hildebrandt demonstrates that the majority of the Gallicisms used by Bolívar were current at that time in the Spanish language and were employed by Garcilaso, Quintana, Moratín, and Jovellanos, among others, and that a great many of them were accepted by the Academy during Bolívar's lifetime or shortly after his death. It also seems from this book that Rousseau did not have much responsibility for the French usages that are present in Bolívar's language, since only two of the Gallicisms of the time have been traced to the writings of Rousseau, *social* and *suculento,* and there is no longer any further possibility that additional ones might yet be discovered. Condillac, Montaigne, Montesquieu, Voltaire, Mirabeau, and others, however, frequently use words that the Liberator carried over into our language and used as if they had already been adopted into the common speech and were the heritage of the times. In spite of all this, Dr. Hildebrandt, in two sections of her work, repeats with

Gil Fortoul that Bolívar "thought" in French and "felt like a true Frenchman"[7]—statements that contradict not only the words quoted from Professor Rosenblatt but also other statements of the author herself, who, after transcribing some paragraphs from a letter in French sent by the Liberator to Alexander Dehollain, holds that "in the French of Bolívar the imprint of Spanish also appears."[8] Thus, according to this account, we would have a Bolívar who thinks in French in order to write in Spanish and thinks in Spanish in order to write in French, a notion which, if not absurd, at least suffers from inconsistency. And this inconsistency will seem all the more extraordinary if we take into account the over-all tendency of Dr. Hildebrandt's book, which is to show that the Liberator uses the Spanish of the America of the eighteenth and nineteenth centuries, such as was "typical of the cultivated man of the epoch of emancipation."

Marius André, a French biographer of Bolívar, in his *Bolívar y la democracia*, falls into even greater error, since in addition to repeating what Gil Fortoul and Mancini say, he attributes too much influence to Simón Rodríguez, through whom he introduces Rousseau and Bolívar's cousin from Paris, Fanny du Villars. At least he concludes by observing that Bolívar shook off all influences and appears with all the brilliance of the creative hero of nations and the liberator of half a continent. But Marius André, whose ideas are basically conservative, is interested above all in stressing in Bolívar those ideas that are opposed to the system of democracy and that have an absolutist tinge.[9]

Dr. C. Parra Pérez, in the Prologue to the second edition of his *Bolívar, contribución al estudio de sus ideas políticas*, is in agreement with the indication of the sources where Bolívar "found ideas favorable to his own tendencies" toward a strong and centralized government, which were no other than those of Voltaire, Rousseau, and the Encyclopedists, corroborated by history. But he also maintained that, while "Bolívar received influences of all kinds, these did not, perhaps on account of their countervailing force and diversity, succeed in eliminating his own originality." The important thing about his Prologue is that Dr. Parra Pérez confesses, "Ten years ago [he was writing in 1928] the author of this book adhered completely to the ideas of Jules Mancini about the intellectual development of Bolívar; imbued with Jean Jacques, Mancini saw his master everywhere. In contrast, we have never attributed to the methods and personal advice of Don Simón Rodríguez the influence that some persons consider decisive in the education of the Liberator and which the Liberator himself flatteringly and emphatically proclaims in a much-quoted letter."[10]

But Parra Pérez, a fervent Mirandist, to whom the noblest studies on the Precursor of Independence, Francisco de Miranda, are due, notes that "from 1810 to 1812 Bolívar held conversations with Miranda, followed his inspirations, and received directly from him the famous sacred fire. In London, he read the letters and the political writings of the illustrious agitator; in Caracas he was one of those who were called 'men of Miranda' in the struggle of the Patriotic Society against the vacillating Congress. The constitutional ideas of the Liberator relating to, for example, the force and vigor of the executive power, essential in his system, are identical with those that Miranda designated in 1795 in his article on the evils that afflicted France and their possible remedies."[11]

Our esteemed friend, Dr. Armando Rojas, in his well-documented work *Ideas educativas de Simón Bolívar,* also follows the path traced by Gil Fortoul and Mancini, and insists on the influence of Rousseau in the development of Bolívar by way of Simón Rodríguez. For Rojas, "many of the ideas of this admirable and at the same time contradictory book [*Emile*] remained floating in the mind of the disciple. Later, when the victorious sword gives way to the pen, Bolívar will find it necessary to expound his ideas about education. Almost a quarter of a century of subconscious dreams fostered these ideas in his mind. Some of them had grown by the light and with the colors of the accent of the old schoolteacher from Caracas. And in the background the smile of Rousseau opens out."[12] However, Rojas notes Rousseau's aversion to the educated woman, who was for Rousseau "the scourge of her husband, of her children and of her friends, of her servants, of everybody," an attitude different from that evinced by Bolívar when he created special institutions for the education of girls and provided for the operation of schools for both sexes.

It is of course true that Rousseau did not wish women to be ignorant altogether and hemmed in solely by household duties, but rather that they be educated so that they "might think, judge, love, know, and cultivate their intelligence in the same way as their figure, which are the weapons given to them by nature in order to make up for the force they lack and to direct our own. They must learn many things," continues Rousseau, "but only those that are suitable for them to know."[13] These sentences speak of a special education for the woman within the framework of her functions as wife and mother, while Bolívar did not propose any such limits, since he enjoyed conversation with cultivated women and thus recommended, in the education of his nephew Fernando, "inspiring him with the liking of cultivated society where the delicate sex exercises its beneficent influence." It will be seen that these ideas are even more opposed to those of Rousseau if one considers that, in another passage on the education of Emile, Rousseau wrote, "Reading, solitude, idleness, a luxurious and sedentary life, the company of women and of youths—these are the dangerous paths that at his age [adolescence] he may walk and that hold him constantly on the verge of danger."[14]

For the aims of this study it is not enough to know the possible influences or the reverberations that certain authors might have had in the general scheme of the Liberator's thoughts, but to indicate concretely, to the degree that it is related to his ideas about education, what was the intellectual inheritance of an age, and what were the forms of culture that spread over everybody and left their mark on everybody, more or less profoundly according to the permeability and malleability of each person.

The dominant ideas of that age came, on the one hand, from the philosophers and thinkers of the *Enlightenment*, from the Encyclopedists and, on the other hand, from those that brought together the process unchained by the *French Revolution*. In the Enlightenment the following ideas stand out: faith in reason, humanitarianism, a blind belief in social progress and in the perfectability of man, and, finally, faith in education, in enlightenment, as the basis for democracy. In the French Revolution the following ideas were predominant: the idea of liberty, the idea of an education that would be official, universal, equally available to all, and free of all dogma.

The thought of Bolívar grew in that ideological soil, but the sprout had its own germinating seed, and the fruits corresponded to the nature and quality of that seed, which in Bolívar generated the liberty of a continent. Perhaps it has been forgotten that Kant had said, "The Enlightenment is the liberation of man from his culpable incapacity. That incapacity signifies the impossibility of using his intelligence without the guidance of someone else. That incapacity is blameworthy because its cause does not reside in the lack of intelligence but in the decision and courage needed to use it without the tutelage of another. *Sapere aude!* Have the courage to use your own reason: here we have the theme of the Enlightenment."[15] But the Liberator knew clearly that a man cannot use his intelligence while exterior forces press down upon him to enslave him. Bolívar's effort toward the liberation of the spirit, teaching it the path of freedom of thought, is his magnificent work of education. "Morality and enlightenment are our first necessities," he said at Angostura, and went on to state immediately thereafter that "an ignorant people is the blind instrument of its own destruction." He did not believe then that enlightenment by itself is enough, because it is possible to have this and, nevertheless, passion or the lack of probity may inhibit the beneficent act or unleash it in a manner damaging to the society. From this observation his dictum, pointing as an index of reproof to a certain kind of injurious intelligence, follows: "Talent without probity is a scourge." Morality was for Bolívar consubstantial with enlightenment.

In this book I maintain that every age has a frame of reference within which men live out their lives; from it they take the values and ideas that they use in order to return them enriched with individual contributions, more numerous and valuable the greater the capacity of the man. Those are the individual contributions to the life of the culture.

One of the most important themes in the educational thought of Bolívar is the tribunal for morality. To be called *Commission on Morals,* it was proposed by Bolívar in the projected Constitution of Angostura as a fourth branch of the government, a moral branch, co-ordinate with the executive, legislative, and judicial branches enshrined in the Constitution of the United States. That organism lends itself to and has been subject to the most varied interpretations. Parra Pérez notes a relationship, which cannot be disregarded, with Miranda's idea of establishing a board of censors "who would oversee public education and assure the conservation of good habits," but that idea is found in

Montesquieu, from whom possibly both took it. It is Parra Pérez himself who observes, as if in passing, that "perhaps Rousseau's ambition to found a natural and lay religion, with dogmas decreed by the State, had been the distant inspiration of Bolívar's project, if one considers that the Genevan philosopher, led to the ultimate consequences that might be deduced from his omnipotent State, allows the justification of all its interventions in all realms of social activity."[16] But Parra Pérez forgets that in the Prologue to the book from which this quotation is taken, he maintains that "Bolívar is not doctrinaire in the way Miranda was." Thus, the idea of a Commission on Morals has nothing to do with Rousseau and his natural religion. I believe that the idea was advanced solely to serve as a counterweight to the all-powerful executive branch defended in the proposal for the Constitution of Angostura, with the aim of correcting a political absolutism with a moral absolutism, and such is the position documented in this essay.

In the analysis presented here, from the texts and references that are provided, it is made obvious that Rousseau had no influence, direct or indirect, on the educational ideas of the Liberator, but rather that there is opposition on that subject between the Genevan and our Liberator. On a question so controversial and of such transcendental importance, I believe that at the very least a myth has been exploded. On the other hand, one must carefully consider the close relationship between the educational thought of Diderot and La Chalotais and that of Bolívar, on account of similarities in language, even though those two names do not appear in any of the numerous works written by the Liberator that we are acquainted with. The vital impact of Montesquieu also stands out in certain constitutional conceptions of the Liberator, as does that of some thinkers of the French Revolution, Condorcet, Talleyrand, and other members of the Convention and of the National Assembly, as well as that of thinkers of earlier epochs in so far as it touches on educational matters.

When did Bolívar begin to concern himself with educational problems? Perhaps it was a concern cognate with his political thought, for the truth is that he could not conceive of democracy without education nor the exercise of liberty by men who came out of slavery completely ignorant of their duties as citizens, something that would make them absolutely incapable of determining the extent of their own rights in confrontation with the rights of others. "Educator in patriotism," Mancini has called him. Parra Pérez says of Bolívar that "his idea of democracy and his own temperament led him to assume the role of leader and educator of peoples."

In spite of all this, it might be thought that Bolívar's concern for education originated during his contact in London with the educator Joseph Lancaster, who, in a letter sent from Caracas on July 9, 1824, recalls to Bolívar how, around September 26 or 27, 1810, in the London house of General Miranda, a sketch of his system "aroused in your mind a lively and powerful interest."[17]

No matter how important that day is considered in which Bolívar, sent as a diplomat to London along with Luis López Méndez and Andrés Bello, displayed "a lively and powerful interest" in a system of ideas about education, which he may have thought appropriate for his America, since within that system the lack of teachers (a quite notable condition in the continent from which Bolívar came) was made up for by employing the older and more advanced students as monitors or auxiliary teachers —such a fact is nothing more than a simple coincidence within which Bolívar's natural inclinations were made evident.

In Bolívar the politician and the educator advance together, intimately and mutually bound together. For him, to liberate and to educate were tasks of the same nature. For that reason, and because he believed "that the most pious works have as their object education, instruction, and public welfare," once the nation of Bolivia was created, he decreed on December 11, 1825, the assignment of certain revenues from Church properties to public establishments, such as those of the important vestries of prebendaries and ecclesiastical courts, confraternities, brotherhoods, revenues of suppressed monasteries and those of ground rents and communities of indigenous peoples. In another decree on the same day, he proclaimed that giving education to the people is "the first duty of the government," that this education should be uniform and general, that the institutions of this nature must abide by the laws of the state, and that the health of the republic depends on the morality which through education the citizens acquire during their childhood. And he provides for the revenues required to maintain educational services, orders the Director General of Education to report on the state of the schools and colleges and on the funds that sustain them, to draw up a plan to create an institution of learning that would embrace all the branches of instruction, making it general for all the people, to establish in each principal city of a district a primary school with the corresponding divisions in order to receive all the children of both sexes of school age, to establish a military school, and to restore the colleges of sciences and arts. On that same day, which would appear to have been a day of educational inspiration, in the midst of concern with his tasks of organizing the new state, Bolívar also decreed the creation of a school for orphans, "in order to avoid the state of abandonment in which many individuals grow up on account of having lost the support of their parents during their childhood." Later, he placed education in Bolivia under the direction of his own teacher, Don Simón Rodríguez.

In order to emphasize his concern for the education of women, along with the idea of the education of mothers, which had been expressed in the Commission on Education proposed in the Project for a Constitution presented by him to the Congress of Angostura in 1819, Bolívar founded in Cuzco a school for girls. The education of girls, he said, "is the foundation of the education of families." That institution was to operate within San Esteban School, "under the authority of the Board of Education of Cuzco, and girls of whatever class who were capable of receiving education were to be admitted, both from the city and from the surrounding district."

These same ideas inspired the creation of the school and academy for girls that he founded in Caracas, the city of his birth, on June 27, 1827, in a decree among whose observations he declared "that the important objective of public education remains very imperfectly realized if the education of girls is not improved."[18]

Now Bolívar's interest in education was not limited to the organization of primary schools and of education offices, but extended to the university. Under colonial regulations, universities had trained people for the professions while hounded by norms that impeded any expansion of education at this level. The Liberator reformed the regulations of the Universities of Trujillo, in Peru, of Caracas, of Quito, and of Colombia, making their administration more liberal and autonomous, but without reforming the curriculum to take in the fresh air of the new science that was transforming institutions and creating the yearning for improvement in the life of our newborn republics.[19] However, he did democratize the universities, making religious, racial, and any other kind of discrimination impossible in them, and he did secularize their administrative personnel.

However, the important thing about Bolívar is not what he wrote about education nor the educational institutions that he created, but the educative influence of his personality, his attitude as instructor, as the leader of an unformed or deformed society, which came to political liberty and to a democratic system of organization without having acquired habits that would support free conduct within an autonomous and just institutional order. Bolívar's labors were directed toward adjusting, within a paternalistic government, the life of Americans so that they might live together in accordance with the law, which is a moderator of the activities of the individual and which tends to shape the conscience of the citizen.

While writing this prologue, a visit that I made to Rivadavia Park, in Buenos Aires, comes back to me. It was a radiant spring day in 1962, full of joyous and noisy people taking the sun after a long winter. At the entrance to the park, the statue of our Liberator standing out on an immense arch of triumph that, in relief carving, presents the Battles of Chacabuco and Ayacucho. On his horse, Bolívar rises in the stirrups as if in a position from which to address an immense multitude. Around this statue children are dancing and singing, climbing over the low pedestal, swaying on the stirrups, which are the swings of glory. The touch of childish hands keeps the legs of the horse shiny, while a good-natured glance descends from the statue over the games of the children.

The children of Buenos Aires talk with the hero, they approach him in a friendly way without any trace of disrespect, and the dialogue next to the trees is a lesson for the future.

I had always thought that the heroes of the statues were unapproachable, distant, and nebulous, and that for this reason we have to take them down from their pedestals, to humanize them in order to set them walking among living men as examples to children and to young men and women, so that in this way their work is prolonged through time as the permanent form of a

teaching that never ends. And this is why I have proposed that
Bolívar be presented to the young as a living and acting man,
free of the rigidity of the statues, and it is just in this way that
I have tried to present him here, with all his ideas and concerns intact, in all his eagerness to serve in which there is no
illusion. Such, then, is the fundamental content of this work,
which might suffer from faults and defects because of the scope
I tried to give it and because of the nature of the researches
undertaken, but in which I believe myself to have indicated a
path of new and promising fruitfulness, which others with more
time at their disposal and with greater skill in interpretation
might be able to achieve.

When this book was already written, Dr. J. L. Salcedo Bastardo
presented me with a copy of a book by Dr. Marisa Vannini de
Geruleviez, *La influencia francesa en Venezuela.* This author emphatically states, "In the case of Bolívar it is necessary to make a
thorough study of his system of ideas. The problem of the
sources of the Liberator's ideas is a living problem that has never
been analyzed as it should be. There are profound and substan-
tial differences between the thought of Rousseau and that of
Bolívar; if we counterpose what is fundamental in the ideas of
Rousseau and of Bolívar, those of the Liberator make it possible
to shape an anti-Rousseau."[20] In this investigation my task has
been precisely this: to prove the existence of opposition between the thought of Rousseau and that of Bolívar with reference to education and, in addition, to show in passing the
existence of such opposition in other realms. However, the field is
extensive. What is difficult is to break the trail so that future
travelers may pass through. It may now be said that the path is
open.

Part One

BOLÍVAR'S LIFE AS AN EDUCATIONAL FORCE

THE PROTEAN ATTITUDE

"Bolívar is like an ocean," said Andrés Eloy Blanco in the National Congress of Venezuela, as he refuted the efforts of those who sought, within the ideas of Bolívar, arguments to justify repressive state actions. The truth is that in Bolívar one may find ideas that inspire and support all the multiple activities of a community in the crisis of transcending itself. For he was a creator of peoples and had to invent out of nothing the systems and services that would make it possible for them to raise themselves to the enjoyment of civilized life, to the right of living as human beings, and to the exercise of the liberty they had won under his guiding action.

For every possible circumstance, for each possible course of action, Bolívar had a solution. This prolific manner of proceeding placed him at the center of a world in turmoil. But, above all, in him the human quality, the capacity for leadership reached such dimensions of excellence that he was converted into an exemplar and model for a whole people, for a whole continent. Bolívar's attitude toward leading and educating exceeds the limits of his own personality. His action as Liberator, which some might think of solely in terms of achieving the independence of nations, is more precisely a wholly liberating action, because it tends to teach men how to use that recently acquired liberty and how to restrain the abuses and excesses of those who, since they are not accustomed to acting freely, run the risk of getting lost along the way.

When one speaks of Bolívar, people think of the great battles that brought liberty to the South American Continent—Carabobo, Boyacá, Junín, Ayacucho, and the thousand other skirmishes where the hero, guiding his people, was himself a people too in the crisis of transcending itself in the struggle against adversity and tyranny. Others see in Bolívar the statesman who founds nations, establishes systems of government, organizes continental congresses, and lays the foundations of a new American legal system, founded on justice and on the equality of the nations of Latin America. Sometimes the man seems to be overshadowed by the hero. People have tried to exalt him into a kind of demigod, forgetting that in that interpretation his actions would lose all meaning, since, if to a god all things are possible, there would then be no merit in converting a world of slaves into a new world of free peoples, nor out of nations without unity and without rights to forge peoples united in the purpose of making justice universal and of extending the field of action of the life of man.

The more human Bolívar is, the greater his worth. His action has meaning as the emanation of a man, of a "human man"—and there is no redundance in this phrase, because inhumanity is an ingredient that usually accompanies the substance of human life.

When voluminous books are written about his life, the hero occupies an extravagant place. Many biographers remain dazzled by the trappings of power and the flash of sabers, if not by the great deeds of singular splendor that fill the existence of the Liberator of America. In contrast to such biographers, I wish to present one aspect of Bolívar's personality, perhaps the most interesting for young students and for the men and women of these lands of ours, all of whom are desirous of receiving the encouragement that may be found in perseverance and faith, in the enduring instructive action that is the educational message of a man whose life was centered in the proposition that his people should adopt a norm of life in their actions and raise up a model worthy of imitation in their attitudes.

We do not begin by speaking of the mischievous Bolívar of the early years, who disregards his teachers and mortifies them all, in spite of their enlightened ways and vast learning, men such as the priest Andújar, the lawyer Miguel José Sanz, Andrés Bello, Simón Rodríguez.

We do not refer to the legend of the world traveler who throws away a fortune in Europe, where he learns languages, cultivates the society of learned men and of politicians, admires Napoleon when he seemed to be spreading the ideas of the Revolution over a continent, and detests him when he crowns himself Emperor; nor to the Bolívar who, taking the hand of his teacher Simón Rodríguez on the Aventine Hill in Rome, surrounded by ruins of the ancient world, swears to consecrate his life and his work to the liberation of his country. For these actions are only the prologue to a life of resolutions that become the source of marvels when he puts himself in contact with his people, when he becomes the very substance of peoples, and when, in constant intimacy with other men, he learns both how to live and how to teach others to live by the principle of dignity in action, generosity in ideas, justice in attitude.

We will devote ourselves to the educational activities of Bolívar, to his labors as a creator of peoples begun in the days of the Patriotic Society. This society was founded in Caracas on August 11, 1810, by the Supreme Junta for the purpose of developing agriculture but was soon converted into the fomenter of emancipationist ideas by the activity of men under forty (Bolívar was then twenty-seven), who initiated the American revolution under the inspiration of the great Girondist, Francisco de Miranda.

Bolívar's educational labors on American principles began in the Patriotic Society. In that society, as all good teachers do, he learns as well as teaches. His overflowing youthfulness, his brilliant and fluent speech, his resolute manner—all bring him to the center of attention of his companions in the assembly, and the people who listen to him regard him as the leader. In the face of the hesitations of the Congress on the issue of declaring independence in 1811, the Patriotic Society serves as a spur and impulse. Coto Paúl invokes anarchy above, remaining in the innervating calm of slavery; Muñoz Tebar, always clear and penetrating, praises the virtues of freedom; but it is Bolívar who pronounces the fiery speech carried as a message to the Congress, expressing unequivocally the longings of the people and the ardent desires of the young. Freedom immediately, without waiting for the outcome of Spain's policy of delay, because for Bolívar "he who hesitates is lost." He pressed for immediate action to lay the foundations of American independence. From that time on, the idea of America as one nation with no limiting frontiers begins to appear in Bolívar, confirmed later in a letter to the Supreme Leader of Buenos Aires and the United Provinces of La Plata, Juan Martín Pueyrredón, in which Bolívar wrote, "The fatherland of all Americans must be one only,"[21] and in all the acts and decisions of his life.

A STATEMENT ON NATURE

The need for that educational labor was driven home following the earthquake that destroyed Caracas in 1812, when the Spanish priests, taking advantage of the innocent credulity and ignorance of the people, predicted lightning and thunder, massive destruction and extermination for the rebels who were the liberators of our people. Bolívar then stood up boldly in an exemplary way to educate the people, in order to restore their faith in liberty, in order to stimulate resistance and to create the will of victorious determination. From an improvised tribunal in the midst of dusty ruins, made out of stone piled upon stone, symbols of the recent catastrophe, he hurled into the face of the astonished dwellers of the martyred city his immortal words, at one and the same time a protest and a warning against the propagandists of the fearsome instinct of conservation: "If nature is opposed to our ambitions, we will struggle against her and we will make her obey us."[22]

Blasphemy, the epigones of tyranny called this bold appeal made by Bolívar to the moral reserves of a people so that they not let themselves be cowed by misfortune. On no other occasion of his stormy life did the educative labors of Bolívar attain greater significance or achieve greater historical understanding. Without thinking it out very deeply, he tried to teach the people that unreflecting fear is destructive, for it depresses creative energies and places the future in jeopardy. Without knowing it, perhaps by the intuition of a great educator of peoples, he expressed the most fruitful lesson of faith in science and in the possibilities of man who knows how to utilize nature in order to vanquish it and bring it into the service of man.

For the truth is that the history of civilization and of culture is nothing but the dramatic struggle of man against nature in order to make it obey. Had man lacked the will to dominate the natural elements, humanity would have remained imprisoned in the nets of barbarism. Thanks to this iron will, the lightning that is tamed does not annihilate, the torrent is channeled through the sluice gates and becomes the source of energy for creation, the mountain that is drilled through offers passage to the desires of men, climate is moderated, the fertility of soils is modified, the force of unleashed elements is restrained, deserts are converted into cities and gardens, and buildings raised on antiseismic foundations absorb the destructive power of earthquakes. Man has grown in liberty to the degree that he has mastered nature, placing it at his service, and from being an implacable enemy he goes on converting it into an ally.

Bolívar, before a people made small and narrow by ignorance which is the inheritance fatally passed on by long centuries of oppression and servility, expressed a lesson in optimism, of faith in the creative energies of man to achieve freedom.

In the hour of greatest danger, in the midst of disaster, the leader has to raise himself above the disintegrative forces; and that is something our Liberator knew how to do in a near-perfect way. "My devotion does not weaken but is even fortified in adversity," he said to Sir Robert Wilson.[23] For that reason, General Pablo Morillo, who had been sent from Spain to put down the rebellion in New Granada, came to consider him most to be dreaded in defeat, because out of it he regained all the forces of his genius and, vanquishing the weaknesses of his condition and those of his soldiers, he incited that heroic will to victory which is the enduring appeal of the teacher, of the guide, in order to raise man to the heights of all his possible aspirations.

The process of education of men and of peoples manages to overcome natural human weaknesses even while respecting them, and teaches how to confront powerful surrounding elements with all the resources of intelligence, in order to construct out of those elements, and at times in spite of them, a civilization. To give battle to nature, to master it, putting it at the service of humanity, is the labor of the educated man. All education implies apprenticeship in that liberating necessity.

Bolívar's malediction against obscurantism and barbarism opened for his people, not the path of flight through an obliging Red Sea, but the path of freedom achieved with exertion and sacrifice, a difficult stretch through which we have come struggling. And we will continue the march until we arrive at the definitive conquest of the inhospitable nature that now dominates our continent and, in this way, achieve complete liberation, not only from subjugation by other peoples, but also from hunger, misery, and lack of culture, which are our traditional internal enemies.

THE LESSON OF CARTAGENA AND THE AMAZING CAMPAIGN

When independence was declared in 1811, and Francisco de Miranda was made leader of the republic, Bolívar enlisted in the army of the nation. The almost immediate defeat of the First Republic surprised him and left him with bitterness in his soul. The treason of the Venezuelan Francisco Fernández Vinoni had led to the fall of one of the major bastions of national resistance, the Castle of San Felipe, at Puerto Cabello, which was under Bolívar's command.

After the First Republic had fallen, Bolívar went to New Granada and there wrote the celebrated Proclamation of Cartagena, in which he analyzed the causes of the disaster. For Bolívar the fundamental cause was the adoption of a federal constitution at a time when what was needed was the consolidation of power in order to bring it to bear on the amassed forces of the Spanish Crown. This proclamation, addressed to the citizens of New Granada, is an instructive lesson in political clarity, explaining to a people how they might avoid falling into the errors that had set back the liberation of Venezuela.

"The federal system," the Liberator said, "although it may be the most perfect and the most capable of apportioning human happiness in society, is nevertheless the most opposed to the interests of our states just now coming into being; generally speaking, our compatriots are still not found in a condition to exercise their rights for themselves and to exercise them in a complete way, since they lack the political virtues that characterize the true republican, virtues that are not acquired under absolutist government, in which the rights and responsibilities of the citizen are unknown." Later on, he continued, "On the other hand, what country of the world, no matter how moderate and republican it might be, in the midst of internal factional struggles and an external war, could be ruled by a government as complicated and weak as a government organized on federal principles is? It is not possible to preserve it in the tumult of battles and divisions. It is necessary that the government, if one might say it like this, identify itself with the character of the circumstances, with the times, and with the people who surround it."[24]

The leader drew an example from the failures and, presenting it to the people, helped them to defend themselves. His idea of adapting government to circumstances was confirmed by the necessities created by the war, and his lesson produced the harvest of our independence.

Further, the proclamation addressed to the people of New Granada and the proposals directed to their sovereign Congress as well sought to gather resources for the invasion of Venezuela. When he had obtained these resources, he organized an army of resolute men, ready to follow him, in spite of the petty jealousies promoted by Manuel Castillo and others in New Granada who were still incapable of understanding that the fate of New Granada was intimately united with the fate of Venezuela, because as long as the power of the Spaniards was not destroyed throughout the continent, the liberty of each and every one of its peoples would remain in danger. With the Venezuelans José Felix Rivas, Vicente Campo Elías, Rafael Urdaneta, the New Granadans Antonio Ricaurte and Atanasio Girardot, and another handful of valiant officers, he crosses the Andes and puts the enemy to flight from his country. This is the *Amazing Campaign,* amazing as much on account of its conception and realization as because it established the liberty of the republic.

His lofty educational process went on sowing consciousness. Those who yesterday were on the side of the Royalists, since they lacked a clear conception of the Venezuelan homeland, learned this devotion from Bolívar. From Bolívar they learned the fervor that converted each man into a citizen and each citizen into a soldier ready to defend his country in order to achieve liberty.

THE PAINFUL BIRTH OF THE NATION

In the minds of those who populated our land, a clear consciousness of Venezuelan nationality did not exist. The war against Spain seemed to be a war of brother against brother, even while the atrocities of the Antoñanzas, the Suazolas, the Rosetes, the Morales spread panic and inundated the fields of Venezuela with Creole blood. Bolívar's educational purpose takes the terrible decision to write the spiritual birth of the nation in blood. Later on Nietzsche was to say, "Write with blood, for blood is the spirit."

On June 15, 1813, in Trujillo, Bolívar issued the dreadful but necessary Proclamation of War to the Death: "Spaniards and Canary Islanders: count on death, even being neutral, if you do not work actively in the cause of liberty for America. Americans: count on life, even though you may be guilty."[25]

The objective of that decree, concerning the significance and consequences of which such divided and contradictory opinions have been expressed, was to separate the sides on the field of battle, in order to light up, clear on the horizon, the image of a nation coming to birth, to see her finally as a mother offering protection to all her children, whatever may have been their errors, and pursuing and punishing not only the obvious enemy but the potential enemy.

The proclamation was also intended to put up barriers against the ferocity of the Royalists, who were deaf to all pleas for mercy and blind to the horror of shedding innocent blood. However, the teacher may have been in error. Perhaps in order to teach his science he was applying the old method of pedagogy, according to which "he who spares the rod spoils the child"; still he cannot be accused of wanting to harm the student who is learning. Bolívar, the great educator of peoples, proclaimed this decree, as José Manuel Restrepo will say, "not out of cruelty and hardness of heart, but out of a systematic approach formed after profound meditation on the character of his compatriots and on the deeds of the Spaniards that had already taken place or that were then occurring in Venezuela even in the regions surrounding him."[26]

The "war to the death" decimated the population of Venezuela, but the noble spirit of Bolívar was always eager to stop the flow of the costly river of blood. He moderated the attitudes of his fellow soldiers, making the reprisals more humane; and a few months after issuing the decree, in December, he set the Spaniards free who had been detained in Santa Fe. And even before then, according to an account given by the Spanish Regent Heredia, on August 4, 1813, less than two months following the proclamation in Trujillo, while in Victoria before entering Caracas, Bolívar offered to the commander of Spanish forces in Venezuela, Domingo de Monteverde, "general reconciliation with complete amnesty for all that has passed, and the right to emigrate for all those who wish it, on condition that they present themselves within one month to request a passport and carry out their departure within another, while being able to give power of attorney to some trusted person in order to look after their interests and finish up their business." This offer was not accepted by Monteverde, who, badly advised, refused to make a pact with those he called "rebels."[27]

In the proclamation of the year 1816, Bolívar projected the humanitarian idea of bringing the "war to the death" to a halt, on condition that the enemy agree—another expression of the spirit with which he sought to implant, not only in the Americans but even in the enemy, the idea that war, as a work carried out by human beings, ought to be inspired by human principles.

In the letter he sent to the American Royalist Juan Bautista Pardo, commander of the Spanish troops in Pampatar on Margarita Island, Bolívar said, "I believe it is my duty to begin this campaign with a great act of humanity, pardoning the prisoners of the maritime forces that blockaded this island and bringing to an end, from our side, the war to the death that dishonors the Spanish nation and desolates America. In consequence, the rights of war will be restored in full force, not excepting those of people who have been observed so horribly violating those rights up to the present." Further on he adds, "The true soldier finds glory only in defeating his enemies, not in destroying them." And in concluding, thinking of that future in which his acts will be a guiding example for his peoples and for the world, he says, "I have reason to fear that posterity will blame me for the blood that is going to be spilled in Venezuela and in New Granada; but I will console myself with leaving the authentic documentation of my love of humanity; and I expect that this will be exact enough to guide the denunciation to those who alone are guilty, the European Spaniards."[28] General Pablo Morillo gave his reply to this generous letter on August 8, 1817, putting a whole village to the knife, in the place that since then bears the name the Lagoon of the Martyrs, on Margarita Island itself.[29]

LIBERATOR, "THE MOST GLORIOUS TITLE"

On August 7, 1813, Bolívar arrived in Caracas, and the people acclaimed him Liberator, confirming the title that had been conferred on him by the city of Mérida.

This was the most treasured of all his honors, for, in spite of the numerous acts of homage that were paid to him by the American nations, he continued to consider this, right up to the time of his death, the most precious thing he had achieved in his life. When some of his associates tried to tempt his vanity in order to force him to place a crown on his head, he recalled this homage of Caracas and Mérida, the prize of his educative work as a leader, and, repudiating the crown, he wrote to General José Antonio Páez, "I am not Napoleon, nor do I wish to be; neither do I wish to imitate Caesar, and even less Iturbide. Such examples I consider unworthy of my own glory. The title of Liberator is superior to all those that human pride has been the recipient of."[30] Bolívar's reference to Iturbide is extraordinarily significant, since Augustín de Iturbide was an officer in the Spanish Royalist army in Mexico who joined forces with the revolutionaries only to establish, in 1822, an independent Royalist government in Mexico with himself as Emperor. The following year he was forced into exile, but a year later returned to Mexico and was captured and shot.

Bolívar's message to Páez was a reiteration of the message he had sent to the municipal government of Caracas on October 18, 1813, to thank them for the honor. At that time he said, "Liberator of Venezuela, for me a more glorious and satisfactory title than the scepter of all the empires of the earth."[31] But in the spirit of civic humility he came to prefer the title of *good citizen*, the only one that made all those who served the nation equal before the law. For this reason, he said in his message to the Congress of Angostura, "If I merit your approbation, I will have attained the sublime title of *good citizen*, to me preferable to that of *Liberator* which Venezuela has given me, to that of *Pacifier* which Colombia has given me, and to all that the entire world may be able to give."[32] He returned to this thought in the speech he gave before the Congress of Colombia, meeting in the Villa del Rosario in Cúcuta: "I wish to be a citizen so as to be free and in order that everybody may be free. I prefer the title of *citizen* to that of *Liberator* because this latter comes from the war, while the former comes from the law. I would exchange all my titles, gentlemen, for that of *good citizen*."[33]

Men who do not know how to be contented within the limits indicated by their merits, who try to raise themselves proudly above their people, climbing upon pedestals for the sake of vain ostentation, might find in Bolívar's conduct a permanent lesson of considered equilibrium, which would be at the same time a reply to the flatterers who blow into their ears in order to inflate their presumption, but which men of genius and of good heart know well enough to refute immediately in order not to compromise in the present the future recognition of the virtues they truly do possess and of the services they really have performed.

SERMONS AND EXAMPLES
FOR THE PEOPLE

Over the ruins of the First Republic, Bolívar began again to initiate organization. The generals who worked with him, the captains of the enterprise, were not always up to their responsibilities. Passion for command, instincts of revenge, and regional jealousies kept getting in the way of unified action, while a reactionary force was concentrated in the Plains under the leadership of Boves, who was again trying to put an end to the republic. Boves, born José Tomás Rodríguez, had originally tried to join the revolutionary army but, identified as a smuggler, had been imprisoned and condemned to death. Freed by the Royalists, he raised a guerrilla force of ten thousand men, all on horseback, for the defense of the Spanish Crown and became, for Bolívar, the incarnation of all that was ignorant and evil in the enslaved populace of Venezuela.

Bolívar tried to live among his men: he ate the food they did and suffered the same hunger, he slept under the open sky, he sang and danced with them, he nourished their joys, soothed their impetuous furies, exalted their virtues, revived the disheartened, supported the weak; he was a hand to wipe away the tears of mothers who wept for their sons lost in combat, protection for the unfortunate, a light to the poor. From his own great wealth he gave to the dispossessed, and from the properties confiscated from the Royalists he secured goods for the army and repaired the damages to the cities and their inhabitants caused by the devastating war.

A center of generous action, he was also an example of sacrifice. He lived in community with all, and his life revolved around the struggle for justice. Because, to him, justice was more important than victory. "Justice," he said, "is the kingdom of republican virtues, and by it equality and liberty are sustained."[34] And, in order to shape the action of his lieutenants and restrain their ambitions, he taught, "It is not military despotism that will make the people happy, nor can the authority that is given to me be advantageous to the Republic, except on a temporary basis. A fortunate soldier does not acquire any right to rule his country. He is the arbiter neither of legislation nor of government; he is the defender of its freedom. His glories must be fused with those of the Republic, and his ambition must remain satisfied with bringing about the happiness of his country."[35]

Rufino Blanco-Fombona, one of the Liberator's most diligent biographers, has stated, "To preach by example, that is a great virtue; to educate men for advancement, that is a great task. Bolívar achieved both these things." And he added, "This apostle of democracy educated people both through preaching and by example."[36]

TEACHING HOW TO BE HEROIC

The war in Venezuela was lost, but among the hoofs of the horses of the men of the Plains it was won. Boves, pushing from the Plains, at the head of his valiant soldiers, destroyed the Second Republic more on account of the lack of unity among the military leaders of the Revolution, deaf to the Liberator's exhortations, than because of the power concentrated in his armies.

Bolívar, in order to exorcise the disaster, exhausted himself in the effort to arouse the will to survive uncaptured. He stimulated faith and resistance. To General Rafael Urdaneta, situated in the city of Valencia, key to communications with the coast and with the Plains, road of access to Caracas, he sent an imperious order: "Defend Valencia, citizen General, to the death; because, since all our elements of war are there, if it is lost, the Republic is lost."[37] It was a heroic teaching, which faithful students knew how to live by, for they were instructed by the example of a teacher who held back no sacrifice in order to create a country, in spite of all those who, beguiled by promises or confused in their purposes, fought under the banners of the King, waved by Boves and his lieutenant Morales.

Camped in San Mateo, the location of the huge estate of the Bolívar family, the merciless soldiers of Boves pressed against the flanks of the patriotic army. The salvation of the nation called for sacrifices. There was no other course but to die or to win. At that point, in order to inflame the passion for liberty and love of country, and to mobilize the spirit of sacrifice, Bolívar unsaddled his horse, with a gesture like that of Cortez when he destroyed his ships in order to make flight impossible, and embracing the neck of the animal, exclaimed, *I will be the first to die here.*

Boves's men surmounted the hill where the patriotic army was encamped, watched over by the young New Granadan officer Antonio Ricaurte, also ready to be the first to die, in order to make of Bolívar's example a perennial lesson of history. A detonation, smoke, and dirt carried a great distance brought the news of the blowing up of the powder magazine, the deed of its defender, and with that act the precipitous flight of the besieging troops.

The educational labors of Bolívar struck fire in souls, in order to ignite a corner of America with glory.

But Boves had not been defeated. Powerful, he threatened to go as far as Caracas and to cover it with desolation and death. In the face of the fear of the presence of Boves in the capital, Bolívar organized the withdrawal to the eastern part of the republic in order to continue fighting. Along sunny and dusty roads, more than ten thousand men and women died without reaching their destination. In the midst of the catastrophe, Bolívar kept on teaching how to resist and how to hope. He mated the virtues of men with faith. Out of that heap of ragged and famished people, he created an army that perished under the knife in the village of Aragua, near Barcelona, and on the plains of Urica, where Boves, the bloodthirsty commander of the Royalist armies, also lost his life, at the hands of a patriotic soldier.

ANTILLEAN PILGRIMAGE

And once again to reorganize armies on foreign soil for the reconquest of the nation. The nation is inside him; it is the substance of his life; where he goes it goes.

He makes the round of the Antilles; he unifies disparate groups and, in the face of the grudges borne by commanders without vision, begins again to assert his sense of educational needs in order to bring them to accept the postponement of their quarrels and their regional ambitions and to put everything at the service of the nation. His educational mission was not only among the Venezuelans, it was among all the people who shared daily life with him and who learned from him to value generous ideals, in the service of which wholeness of will and sacrifice are more important than many resources in the hands of those who are unable to utilize them in works of creation, justice, and freedom. "He who gives up everything in order to be useful to his country," Bolívar said, "loses nothing, and gains as much as he bestows."[38]

Many years later he wrote to José de Sucre, the disciple in

whom the seed of light most profoundly took hold, "Glory is to be great and to be useful."[39] That letter to Sucre, who complained of having been slighted in being sent to organize the rear guard of the army, is a beautiful lesson of the great teacher of peoples. "The assignment I have given you," he continued, "is something I wanted to take care of myself, but thinking that you would do it better than I could, on account of your tremendous capacity for work, I conferred it on you more as a proof of preference than as a humiliation. You know that I do not know how to lie, and you also know that the pride of my soul never degrades itself in feigning. Thus you must believe me." The disciple absorbed the lesson and understood that the resentment he had shown was a result of his own thoughtlessness. The teaching of faith generated magnificent efforts that culminated soon thereafter in Ayacucho, the crucial battle, led by General José de Sucre, representing the summit of glory that sealed the independence of America.

In his Antillean pilgrimage, in the search for material resources with which to continue the struggle, Bolívar knocked at all doors. In Jamaica he scattered his ideas in the press and explained the causes of the defeats his nation had suffered. "Disunity," he said, "is often the thermometer of freedom. The enjoyment of a government to which free consent is given is usually found in direct proportion to the turbulence of parties and to the clash of political opinions. It is true that the weight of liberty is slight, but it is also true that it is difficult to maintain it in equilibrium even in the most cultivated and civilized nations." And he adds, "Our discords have their origin in two overflowing sources of public calamity: ignorance and weakness. Spain fomented one of them through superstition and perpetuated the other by its tyrannies."[40]

This sociological explanation was an argument directed toward securing protection for weak and forsaken peoples, "whose bandaged eyes" made it impossible for them "to see justice and still less to hear the truth." Acutely conscious of having been abandoned by all, he concluded, "We do not have any weapons to confront the enemy with other than our bare hands, our bodies, our horses, our lances."

In addition to this, the Liberator set himself the task of explaining the conduct of the New Granadans, who were entangled in civil strife that worsened the already existing divisions, creating a favorable occasion for invasion by the Spanish forces under General Morillo. The educator pointed out the causes of the discord and, in order to combat them, proposed the uniting of forces, because "when the groups are without authority, whether because of lack of power or because of the triumph of their adversaries, discontent is born and it debilitates them."[41]

In a moving letter sent from Kingston, Jamaica, to Maxwell Hyslop, he paints the anguish in which Venezuela and New Granada were living, refers to the well-equipped reinforcements received by the troops of General Morillo, increased by contingents of unreflecting Creoles. All this, according to Bolívar, was due to the fact that "the opinion of America is not yet well formed, and although those who think are all of them wholly independent, the general masses are still ignorant of their rights and are not aware of their own interests." He concludes, saying, "It is already time, sir, and perhaps this is already the last time in which England can and must take part in the fate of this immense hemisphere, which is going to succumb or be exterminated if some powerful nation does not offer its support in order to sustain this continent in the act of disengagement that it is now to be found hurled into by its own mass, by the vicissitudes of Europe, and by the eternal laws of nature. Perhaps a little help in the present crisis would be enough to prevent South America from suffering cruel devastation and enormous loss of life! Perhaps when England tries again to look toward America, it will not find it!"[42]

In Jamaica he very nearly lost his life at the hands of a slave paid by the Spanish Government, but this did not intimidate him. It was there that he wrote his famous "Letter to an English Gentleman," usually called the Jamaican Letter, a clear-sighted document in which his vision as a leader indicates the future destination of our peoples, reviews their failures and disappointments, and determines what remedies and precautions are advisable in order to counteract the consequences that arise out of the geographic, economic, political, social, and cultural state of chaos.

The whole document, which is a perfect affirmation of geopolitics at a time when this science had not yet revealed its consequences for warfare and even less for peace, seeks as its objective to draw attention to America and to raise the resources needed to continue the struggle for freedom. The propagation and diffusion of ideas are the educative way to a diversity of influences, and Bolívar understood and used this method with the deliberate purpose of preparing the minds of others to receive his work. In that document he said, "We expected, with good reason, that all civilized nations would rush to help us, so that together we might achieve a favorable state of affairs whose advantages would be reciprocal between both hemispheres. However, what frustrated expectations! Not only the Europeans, but even our brothers of the North have held themselves aloof as unmoving spectators to this conflict that, by its very nature, is the most just and, by reason of its consequences, the most important and magnificent of all those that have been provoked in ancient or modern centuries—for, how far is it possible to calculate the transcendent consequences of the liberation of the hemisphere of Columbus?"[43]

Not all doors were closed to this call for help expressed by Bolívar. Haiti, the black nation recently freed from the colonial power of France, was an open heart where there was room for the desires of our peoples to gain their freedom. In Haiti, the memory of the struggle for freedom was still alive, and the imprint of the broken chains still remained. Bolívar's appeal for generous support from Alexandre Pétion, President of Haiti, found a favorable echo, and in response to Bolívar's unwritten agreement to grant liberty to the Negro slaves of Venezuela and of all the freed lands of America, the Haitian President supplied arms and munitions for the liberating venture. To this magnanimous act was added the collaboration of Luis Brión, the arms merchant of Curaçao, who offered Bolívar a flotilla of small craft for a new invasion of the Venezuelan coast, a mission known in history as the "Expedition of Les Cayes," from the name of the place in Haiti from which it set out.

And again the struggle against disunity, against the deceptions of the priests, against those who would confine the nation to the boundaries of their own province or to the distance of a day's ride on horseback. But, over them all, finally triumphant, are the guiding will of Bolívar, his directing action, his educating labors, which utilize weaknesses, which build, by the force of example, the ideal of a republic for all. In a letter from Port-au-Prince dated November 26, 1816, he wrote to the priest of the cathedral in Caracas, José Cortés de Madariaga, "On the eve of departing for Venezuela, I take advantage of the opportunity to send you my latest words. Up to this moment I have not been able to put my affairs in order, because when means are scarce, obstacles multiply; but finally I depart with the hope of seeing you very soon in the heart of our country, co-operating effectively in the construction of the great edifice of our republic. In vain do weapons destroy the tyrants if we do not establish a political order capable of repairing the ravages of the revolution. The military system is that of force, and force is not government: thus we have need of our eminent men who, having escaped on timbers from the shipwreck of the revolution, may guide us through the reefs to a port of salvation. You and our friends Roscío and Castillo would make a fraud of the Republic if you did not devote your virtues and your talents to it, for remaining inactive would be very prejudicial to the public cause."[44]

This conciliatory appeal, directed to the enlightened mind and to the eminent virtues of our great men, who were heroic in their capacity for service, will be seen to have been much more important at that moment than it may appear to have been, if one considers the embittered struggle that had to be avoided in order to bring the expedition together, for in it the passions of dissension and the question of who was to be in charge were aroused in Francisco Bermúdez and his partisans. But the great educative labors of Bolívar took on the outlines of sublime expression in difficult hours, as he tried to persuade men to participate honorably in the work of national liberation that he had undertaken. If he sometimes showed that he could be severe, it was because he considered exemplary punishment necessary, such as occurred in the case of the insubordinate General Manuel Piar. He let Piar hang because he was guided by the purposes of emancipation, which his captains were unable to understand completely, but which he was obliged to make them acquire, by intuition if necessary. For that reason, on the occasion of the disputes with Bermúdez, with Mariño, with Páez, with Rivas, with Arismendi, he assumed an attitude of reproach or of tolerance, according to how it might suit the interests of the country and according to the necessities created by his position as leader. In order to alleviate regional quarrels among the leaders that threatened to divide the army and bring down the republic, he interposed his directing function as mediator. His great and beneficial educational labors sought to reconcile those who were accomplishing the work of national liberation, bringing them together in a common effort. That purpose was behind his conciliating intervention to settle the dispute over precedence between Santiago Mariño and Juan Bautista Arismendi, or the differences between Cumaná Province and the island of Margarita. He wrote to Mariño, Supreme Leader of Oriente Province, warning of the danger of a civil war between provinces, which would be fomented by the enemy as being in their interest and to their benefit, but which could be avoided by making the necessary sacrifice of the adornments of pride.[45] And to Arismendi he argued, "If good understanding between leaders is under ordinary circumstances necessary and at all times useful, it is at the present time indispensable in the face of the advantages (not, however, of great moment) that our enemies have obtained in the province of Barinas and to the west of it."[46]

OVER THE BACKLANDS
OF THE ORINOCO

The republic wandered insecurely from encampment to encampment. It was sustained by lances raised like a forest over the scorched land of the Plains and maintained in wakefulness by the sword of Bolívar, until he arrived one day riding over the backlands of our great river, the Orinoco, dismounted on its bank, and sat down to dream of victory. He began diligently to legislate for freedom, and there grew in him the desire to cross mountains in order to seed himself nobly, beyond the Andes, in a confederated feeling of great nationhood, with two oceans as boundaries.

From Guayana, named provisional capital of the republic, Bolívar organized the reconquest of the country and the liberation of New Granada, where Morillo, with cruel obstinancy, had destroyed and annihilated every stronghold of liberty. From Guayana, with Bolívar at its head, the army set out, going back

up the Orinoco and the Apure, in quest of victory for the Plains
of Apure and Calabozo. Upon the immense tapestry of the treeless plains, the hoofs of the cavalry of Páez, of Zaraza, of Cedeño
sounded as if over a tightened drum, as a summons to combat.
They went in search of the heart of Venezuela, overflowing with
enthusiasm. There Bolívar got to know Páez; there he put his
teaching skill to work among the humble men of the Plains, in
order to awaken them in friendly comradeship to confidence in
victory and faith in the destiny of the republic, thinking on a
grand scale, outside the confines of their rivers, beyond the
horizon that reached their eyes or that could be measured by the
pace of their animals. Man to man with them, he won their
trust, which he was always able to inspire in the hearts of the
humble. Daniel F. O'Leary, who joined Bolívar's cause at the age
of eighteen, tells us, "Generals, commanders, and officers, with
respect to manner of living, were on an equal footing even with
the common soldier; they participated in the same details, ate
the same rations, water, and meat, prepared in the same way.
Even including uniforms all were equal, so that even the Liberator did not wear on the Plains any distinctive uniform at all.
There were even times when he was short of clothing."

In pursuit of victory, they fell on Morillo at Calabozo, but he,
following one defeat, was able to evade further combat and
abandoned the site with an able strategy. Afterward, the army
of the republic penetrated the fertile valleys of Aragua, surrounding Caracas, cradle of the revolution, to return battered from
the horrendous Battle of La Puerta, place of death for the hopes
of the republic.

And again Guayana, splendid Guayana, offers the hero its encouraging protection. Bolívar was able to wait there, while the
river rose and fell, and the ships of Admiral Brión carried out
reconnaissance missions for him. Instead of desperation, what
grew in Bolívar was faith in ultimate victory, because he
had justice on his side and he was fighting for freedom against
oppression. He gave himself over to organizing the republic,
hoping that the respectability of his purposes would produce the
impact of prestige among the watching powerful nations, who
saw a continent bleeding to death without offering their help,
and trying to subdue, through the organization of a government

with laws and elected authorities, the harsh individuality of the military leaders, who raised up little nations within the boundaries of their encampments, at the same time that Bolívar was trying to form, out of the many-colored remnants of these little nation-states, the whole cloth of the great nation that would encompass all.

A LESSON IN OPTIMISM

Hallucination or delirium of Casacoima, this is what history calls the Bolivarian notion of liberating America by beginning on the banks of the Orinoco. Madness, that is how his lieutenants spoke of the enterprise, which they heard him express, still dripping with swamp water, following a ducking at the place where the Orinoco forms the lagoon of Casacoima, a name that in Spanish rings of the gambling house.

A Royalist squad surprised Bolívar, caught unawares with a group of officers. The others fled over dry ground, but Bolívar, in order to save his life, dove into the lagoon, and when he reached the other side, a mile away, while the Spanish patrol was still looking for the republican officers, now sheltered in a ramshackle farmhouse, with an air of determination and in a voice of certainty, absolute master of his dreams, he taught a lesson of faith in the American future to the handful of warriors who accompanied him, saying to them, "I left Les Cayes in the company of only a few officers, without any resources but hope, promising myself to go from one end of the country held by the enemy to the other and to conquer it. I have realized half of my plans; we have overcome all obstacles to arrive at Guayana. In a few days we will subdue all the Royalists in this region, and then we are going to liberate New Granada and, throwing our enemies out of the rest of Venezuela, we will establish Colombia. Then we will raise our flag over the volcano Chimborazo and go on to complete our work of liberating South America and securing our independence, carrying our victorious pennants into Peru. Peru too will be free."[47]

That lesson of faith took hold of their spirits, and all of them, invigorated by the fire of that liberating passion, felt not only that their clothing had been dried but that confidence in victory had been reborn in them.

Bolívar grew under adversity. He was not able to become disheartened, because everybody expected stimulation and leadership from him. He was borne up by his faith in the destiny of America, and his passion for freedom was the inspiration of his efforts and of his speeches with which he sowed in his followers the same order and the same willful energy, thrown wholly against adversity. Perhaps the dream of Casacoima, which was an ideal plan of redemption, reinspired him at difficult moments. On that account, perhaps, when the Andes had already been crossed and in the midst of an uncertain struggle to consolidate the freedom of Peru, sick and battered, in the middle of the quicksands of the Peruvian deserts near Pativilca, surrounded by powerful enemies against whom he was able to oppose only a diminished army with scarcely a weapon and with hardly any provisions, to the question asked of him by the great New Granadan patriot, Don Joaquín Mosquera, "What are you thinking of doing now?" he responded without hesitation, "To win! . . . As soon as I get my health back I'm going to Trujillo. If the Spaniards come down out of the mountains to look for me, I will beat them absolutely with my cavalry, and if they do not come down, within three months I will have enough force to attack. I will go up the mountains and I will rout them."[48]

History knows that he kept this promise, which is the lesson of permanent optimism given to our peoples. A short time later occurred Junín and Ayacucho, the final battles of the struggle for American independence, and the beginning of the great battle to win the peace on a continent that had grown accustomed to warfare as the only form of existence. Bringing about the transition from the regimented encampment to civil life under the rule of law, where the supreme power does not rest on the range of artillery but on the scope of justice, was a fierce struggle that embittered his life and brought him to his death.

INSTRUCTIONS FOR HIS LIEUTENANTS

Creative leader par excellence, Bolívar employed his marvelous faculties to develop in his lieutenants, in the men charged with the tasks of liberation, the aptitudes required for service in war and in peace. That work of educating was never forsaken by Bolívar. In his acts and in his correspondence opportune suggestions on how to achieve an effective performance of duty are always to be found, whether concerned with how to prepare for battle and how to win each battle, how to edit a newspaper, how to write a message, how to fulfill a diplomatic assignment, how to shoe horses or to tame them or acclimatize them, how to make adequate use of weapons, and even how to carry oneself in society or at the table.

Blanco-Fombona, with his passionate and considerable admiration for Bolívar, points out this creative virtue in the great leader of peoples which, out of nothing, builds whatever of action, of thought, of material, of life was indispensable to the fulfillment of his grand continental tasks. For us that creative capacity is consubstantial with all educative work, which precisely in the realm of habits formulates the principles of new behavior. Bolívar was compelled to create the active virtues of the free citizen in minds benumbed under the weight of slavery. He had to create the appropriate frame within which that activity might be developed. The frame emphasizes the picture, bringing out its values. That is why Bolívar hammered out the institutions— as a frame within which the ardors of the citizen are contained and where each person has an opportunity to fulfill his duties and to struggle for his rights. Alluding to those functions, Blanco-Fombona said of Bolívar, "Public opinion does not exist; he creates it. Constitutions do not exist; he writes them. Administration is unknown; he establishes it.

"He taught General Azuola one day how to draw up a message; General Heres, how to manage a newspaper; General Sucre, what iron he ought to employ in the manufacture of nails and what for cartridge cases; General Páez, how to guard a herd of horses with a few people; the lancers of the Plains, how to fight with a rifle; the Congressmen of 1819, how they should educate the future leaders of the nation and how, in time of peace, only public education and European immigration could make the country prosper.

"Out of the colony, he created the Republic; out of a horde, an army; out of anarchy, public order; out of slavery, freedom; out of humiliation, democracy."[49]

In his *Diario de Bucaramanga*, L. Perú de Lacroix tells about the kindness with which Bolívar invited to his table, in order to teach him good manners, the recently risen officer Freire, who had all the habits of a soldier, unsuited, according to the narrator, to occupy a place at the table of the President of the Republic. Nevertheless, the Liberator admits him, indicating a place, and, even when, after the meal he acknowledges the rustic nature of the military staff officer, he still orders "that he come every day to lunch and dinner; we may use up all our provisions, but we will take the rough edges off him and teach him good manners."[50]

In that conduct of the great man the primal form of educational action was present, already made evident with the plainsmen in the encampments, with his companions at arms in the normal relations between chief and subordinates. It is the conduct he assumes in prescribing to Colonel Tomás de Heres the attitude he ought to follow as a diplomat, reiterating, so that he not forget the essential part of the advice, "In diplomatic affairs, I will give you a good maxim: calm, calm, calm; delay, delay, delay; compliments, vague words; consultations; examinations; misconstruing of arguments and of demands; references to the new Congress; digressions on the nature of the issue and the character of the documents, and always much coolness, and much brevity in order not to give away anything of value to your adversary." Farther on he added, "Above all, hold yourself always firm in the highest principles and in universal justice . . . We will act for the right and leave it to time to work miracles."[51]

The highest principles, right action, and time are the instruments of educational work, and Bolívar prescribed them to others and utilized them in his own work of human creation, destined to live and grow in the future. With what composure he set himself the task of changing the ways of behavior of his fellow citizens! He knew that, in order to be free, men must learn to live together and to respect one another, and he did not stint in the efforts directed toward affirming the effects of law and order for those who, without the necessary preparation, threatened a coup in the midst of democracy. "The soul of a servant," he had said in the "Jamaican Letter," "rarely comes to value a healthy liberty; he infuriates himself in tumults or he humiliates himself in chains."[52] Later on he repeated and amplified these ideas in the Message of Angostura. There he affirmed, "A perverted people, if they gain their freedom, very quickly lose it again; because one will struggle in vain to demonstrate to them that happiness consists in the practice of virtue, that the rule of law is more powerful than the rule of tyrants, since it is more inflexible, and everybody has to submit to its beneficent rigors, that good habits and not force are the tablets of the law, that the army of justice is the army of freedom."[53]

We lacked those habits of civilized life that are achieved only through the settling down and patient accommodation of each citizen to his tasks, in which man is educated for service to the community. That was the way of putting education into action carried by the thought of the Liberator with so much concern.

PEOPLING THE DESERT

Bolívar knew, as all good teachers do, that the educational process is slow and that one does not learn to be free except by patiently entering into activity and contention. For that reason, speaking with desperate anguish, but secure in his judgments and learned in the history of all peoples, he said to Commodore Hull, "These countries will be unable to progress for the first hundred years; it is necessary that two or three generations pass away. It is necessary that immigration from Europe and from North America be fostered in order to establish the sciences and the arts here. With this, and with independent government, free schools, and marriages with Europeans and Anglo-Americans, the character of the people will change and they will be free and happy."[54]

Many years later these same words were to spark the polemics
in Argentina between Juan Bautista Alberdi and Domingo Faus-
tino Sarmiento about establishing the priority of education over
immigration or vice versa, one over the other, when what Bolívar
had already said was that one must be joined to the other so that
together they might pave the road to civilization.

The war depopulated Venezuela, which lost a great proportion of its inhabitants. In such a situation, to fill the desert was
a civilizing task, and even more so if one considers that education
and culture do not prosper in solitude, but are affirmed in the
contact of peoples and of men bound together in common purposes. That is why Bolívar spoke in favor of immigration from
Europe and North America, to bring about an increase in population, "once order and the foundations of the governments with
armed forces, public opinion, and foreign relations have been
established."[55]

THE PEOPLE, MALLEABLE CLAY

Bolívar, as we have already seen, lived among the plainsmen.
He studied their ways and found that this portion of people,
who had followed Boves in order to destroy the republic, were
a malleable clay in the hands of a great artificer, and put to work
his talents and his noble educational labors, and out of those
men he improvised an army that, crossing the lofty plateaus
over impossible slopes, won victories at Gámeza and Pantano
de Vargas and brought liberty to New Granada at the Bridge
of Boyacá. While ascending the heights, Bolívar was shaping in
them the characteristics of a great people, who in a glorious gesture of generosity unfasten chains and build free nations the
whole length of a continent "where before tyranny had ruled."

In order to understand the exemplary attitude of the leader
who, at the side of his people, constructs the courageous theory
of the nation marching toward glory, one would have to read the
fascinating account given by O'Leary, who was a contemporary
eyewitness. "Incidents," writes O'Leary, "multiplied and seemed
to unite in order to drown Bolívar's hopes, who was the only

one who always saw clearly in the midst of mishaps, such that the least of them would have been enough to discourage a spirit other than his. He encourages the soldiers, mainly by the force of his own example, but also through speaking to them of the glory that awaits them and of the abundance that reigns in the country they are going to liberate. The soldiers feel happy listening to him and they redouble their efforts." He could not be discouraged, for everybody trusted in him; and around that trust the unformed clay was being molded, the noble clay of the people, capable of destroying a republic if Boves were to lead them or to conquer freedom for a continent if Bolívar guided them. Rough men accustomed to a hazardous life of struggle with the elements, who destroy and kill without knowing the reason, if there is nobody to put into their hands the opportunity for the jealous defense of ideals.

The Colombian writer Indalecio Liévano Aguirre, after pointing out "the extraordinary faculties of the Liberator for gaining the sympathies of people and to awaken with his ideas and his gestures the emotions of people," such as belong to all the leaders of peoples, to the true leaders and educators of masses, attests to the change of attitude that was produced among the plainsmen by the presence of Bolívar among them. "Up to that moment," says Liévano Aguirre, "the masses of horsemen of the plains had been conquered by men who went down to them and, by stimulating their lowest instincts, were able to convert them into the tremendous battering ram that destroyed three centuries of civilization. Such was not the way of Simón Bolívar. His robust Creole personality, his responsibility as a statesman, and his powerful will to dominate, brought him to attempt a venture of superior historical transcendence: to dominate the plainsmen and the plains, imposing his own personality upon them, along with his ambitions and his purposes, showing them their own capacity for realizing the things for which they had followed and were to follow their 'natural' leaders, but leaving them also with the unmistakable certainty that there were superior ambitions and undertakings to be attempted, with the aim of drawing them out of that primitive social stage, where they fought only to rob, to murder, and to get revenge, converting them into a heroic force that would carry the banners of freedom throughout the New World."[56]

That transference of values, that subtle influence that is produced when the leader and his followers are put into contact, is of the essence of education. The leader assimilates the existing values of the community in order to return them transformed through a process of emotional and intellectual maceration, dispersing within them as in a mass of dough the cultural leavening that transfigures the nameless mass, the multitude, into a people with an enlightened conscience, which makes of the simple man in the street a citizen in whom the law shapes conduct and the ideal indicates the direction of his activities.

Bolívar carried out that process of slow purification among his people, and for that reason, as Liévano Aguirre himself states, "little by little the initial doubts of the plainsmen began to disappear, and the staff of the Liberator found the strongest basis of their work in the hearts of those men, who, upon seeing that he was great on account of what he had in common with themselves, began to grow enthusiastic about what was particular to him— his American dreams, his historical ambitions, and his struggle for glory."[57]

And that is the way the people are, unformed clay, until a sculptor comes and shapes them in order to make a statue raised over the Andes to perpetuate the glory and the liberation of a continent. And Bolívar was that artificer. His educative labors were able to make disciplined and loyal soldiers out of rough plainsmen. That Negro, Primero, who dies pierced by a lance in Carabobo, previously a soldier of the royal host, in front of Bolívar was transformed, explaining his crime of service to the Goths, guided by a rage for possessions. When Bolívar questioned him about what had caused him to serve with the Royalists, the magnificent Negro, lowering his head, told him, "Sir, it was greed. I had seen that everybody went to war without a shirt and without one peseta, and that they came back later dressed in a beautiful uniform and with money in their pockets. So I wanted to go to seek my fortune too, and more than anything else to get three sets of silver, one for the Negro Mindola, another for Juan Rafael, and another for myself."[58] Cured of his ambition in the liberating army, Primero learned what the fatherland is and devoted himself to serving it. And this Negro, Primero, who in combat opened up holes in the ranks of the enemy, was clay of that people, sculpted by the educative labors of Bolívar, who are capable of a thousand great deeds according to the quality of the leader. However, Rufino Blanco-Fombona states that the drama of Bolívar "was one of the saddest that history knows of. He was the great man without a great people." Mario Briceño Iragorry, another Venezuelan writer with conservative ideas, speaks of "a crisis of people." In a different work, I have stated that, in my opinion, there has never been nor can there be a crisis of people.[59] There can be a crisis of leaders. The intellectuals charged with leading and teaching the people have failed in their grand ministry, and the people are to be found without direction and without a path and will have to take one worked out for themselves, made by themselves.

In order for the people to grow, in order that they magnify themselves in action, in order that they assume their responsibilities, it is necessary to give them a purpose, to create for them ideals, to lead them, and this task is that of education, of leadership, which the teachers of the present ought fervently to be fulfilling. Bolívar carried out that task, and the portentous work of his educational labors was the independence of half a continent. He is not distinguished from his people, but a part of them, a flower that is raised over the foliage fed by the sap that rises generously from the root. On this account, Blanco-Fombona could say, "Bolívar was assimilated, on account of his heroism, on account of his constancy, on account of his glory, on account of his very disasters, to the nation that marched in his footsteps in ardent throngs."[60] Expressions that contradict what was previously quoted from this same author.

Bolívar never wanted to appear as a superior product separated from his people, because he had a clear consciousness that only a man who identifies himself with the leaders and interprets them is able to lead. Upon that fact and that awareness the success of his educative labors rests. Thus he said, "I have harvested the fruit of all the services of my fellow countrymen, relatives, and friends. I have represented them in the presence of nations and I will represent them in the presence of posterity."[61]

Bolívar's value in the history of America and in the history of Venezuela is that he found an unformed nation and he taught it to spell out an alphabet of liberty; he created laws for it, conquered dignity for it, taught it to serve ends of its own, and, already well on the path toward being a law unto himself, the leader eliminated his own personal powers. He did this so that, as he wrote to Pedro Gaul, "History will say: Bolívar took command in order to liberate his fellow citizens, and when they were free he left them to govern themselves by laws and not by his will."[62] There in a nutshell is the pedagogical function of the work of Bolívar. The teacher trains for a free activity that the student will fulfill by making his own path, realizing his own work, without the permanent walker imposed on him by the will of the teacher. People who were capable of achieving the liberty of a continent, who created free institutions of their own, and forged a destiny of their own in pain and sacrifice, are qualified for the exercise of freedoms, for the performance of democracy, and for that reason do not require constant surveillance, repressive action, the kind of regimentation that makes impossible all authentic expression of popular liberty.

THE STRUGGLE AGAINST ADMINISTRATIVE CORRUPTION

Bolívar's practice of giving examples is of the greatest importance when it comes to the matter of watching over the administration of public funds and their proper disbursement. He found a public treasury that was impoverished by the effects of the war and drained by the unscrupulous actions of administrators.[63] He proposed, on the one hand, increasing taxes and, on the other, channeling their expenditure into useful and necessary activities, while at the same time putting an end to the plundering practiced by those charged with collecting taxes. For the tax collectors frequently became wealthy, in spite of the poverty of the treasury, or squandered in gambling the little taken in, while the people perished in the greatest misery.

The evil practice spread, not only on account of the ignorance of the soldiers, who were accustomed to sacking enemy properties and to disposing of the funds and properties of the state as things of their own, but also on account of unscrupulous leaders, officers, and civil servants. Such was the state of corruption reigning at the time that the Minister of Finance, José Rafael Ravenga, stated, "It was not infrequent to see an officeholder place bets in gambling with sacks holding thirty or forty ounces of gold; some of them have retired with great wealth at the end of a few months; and there has even been a subordinate official who, having entered into service in a state of destitution, has acquired a fortune of more than fifty thousand pesos in less than a year."[64]

This ugly blemish on our public life, which is the crime of embezzlement, Bolívar tried to eradicate through an honest and exemplary circumspection in the management of public funds, so that, seeing his conduct, the administrators might restrain themselves (in this way the educator tries to dam up unleashed passions), or by resorting to severe punishments, including the death penalty, which does away with the guilty and terrorizes possible criminals (in this way the magistrate puts an end to crime).

To this end, Bolívar said to the Congress of Peru, "National finances are in a sorry state of disorder. Some of the offenses against them have been made more serious and have been corrected; terrible punishments have been visited upon agents of the treasury who collaborate in defrauding the public treasury. I know that capital punishment belongs to the realm of cruelty; but the existence of the state is preferable to everything. Thus I have not hesitated to show my severity against those criminals who feed upon the blood of their fellow citizens. The Congress knows that corruption in this sphere penetrated into the very existence of society. For that reason, I have judged it a vital necessity that severe laws be enacted."[65]

In Colombia, where corruption had reached inconceivable limits, since many victorious generals wanted to get paid, outside the stipulations of the law, for the glorious deeds of their swords and their lances, Bolívar held up clean hands so that they might be seen from afar as a notice, as a wind-blown banner on a solitary peak, to the end that others take from his conduct secure guidance in morality and faith. He wrote to one congressman, "To the purpose, or without purpose, I forgot to say to you that I have known that there are some complaints against some public officials. For the government, nothing can be more useful or more satisfactory than to correct the abuse of the administration, because the government wants nothing so much as to see itself supported by the legislators in order to correct the way things are going. That all those who commit infractions be denounced, and that all be punished, myself first of all."[66]

THE PRESS AS A FORCE
FOR PUBLIC VIRTUE

In order to correct the evil, in addition to the law, he trusted in the ethical influences of the press, which is an effective instrument for arousing the vigilance of the public and for creating a sense of responsibility in the citizen, since dissolute behavior, public and private, does not make any distinction between private property and public goods. To rob the treasury, to cheat the government out of the public money, to evade taxes are crimes that can be inhibited and prevented only by the cultivation of a civic pride that is very far from being possessed by recently inaugurated citizens who came out of a state of colonial dependence where those crimes constituted the normal way of acting for the functionaries of the Crown in spite of the severe punishments laid down in the laws and in the judgments sometimes taken against retiring officials. The great fortunes of the colony, and later of the republic, were formed, in the majority of cases, on the basis of that wanton confusion of two different kinds of property: that of the state and that of those charged with guarding it. Such confusion is a weighty inheritance which even now afflicts us, because we still have not achieved that civic pride and that moral consciousness which our Liberator tried so hard to cultivate in us. This fact demonstrates that the lesson of the teacher is not sufficient; there must also be a student disposed to learn and a receptive medium in which the seed can take hold, put down roots, and reproduce itself in fruit.

"Most of the agents of the state," the Liberator wrote to Peruvian patriot Hipólito Unanue, "rob it of its blood, and this should be cried aloud in public papers and on all sides." And farther on he added, "The masters of the mines, the owners of the Andean sources of gold and silver, are asking for millions in loans in order to underpay their little armies and their miserable administration. All this should be communicated to the people, and our abuses and ineptitude should be denounced, so that it not be said that the government shelters the abominable system that is ruining us. Our abuses, I say, should be denounced in the government *Journal,* and such sights should be presented as would wound the imagination of the citizens."[67]

This appeal to the ennobling effects of the press was one of Bolívar's educational resources. From it followed his concern for the creation and circulation of newspapers. Within them, as a simple journalist sometimes, at other times as a teacher, he let fly his ideas. The newspaper was for him a professorship in citizenship, an instrument of propaganda in favor of independence, a weapon against the enemies of the nation and of its laws, a tribunal from which to denounce, as in the case of the offenders against state property, those guilty of that pernicious crime.

Bolívar's teachings, his ideas on the proprieties of public administration, on honesty in the management of public funds, are a lesson of enduring relevance. His teaching seeks permanent realization. It does not aim to apply the death penalty physically, but as a civic death and a public condemnation pronounced by a people of elevated civic spirit and of morally irreproachable conduct, who are the only inexorable judge capable of burying dishonest public officials in opprobium.

THE LESSON OF UNSELFISHNESS

Outside of glory and the love of the people, Bolívar wanted nothing for himself. He had no interest in money; thus the great fortune he inherited was used up in his desire to liberate a continent. In 1821, before the Congress, he gave up the salaries and the rewards that Colombia had bestowed upon him in recognition of his public services. These acts of his are expressions in agreement with his educative mission, founded on unselfishness and the love of service, which are effective ways of behaving for all good teachers, who do not seek personal gain but come closer to realizing the highest good of the people.

"The law of expenditure of the national wealth," said Bolívar to the Congress, "has assigned me an income of 25,000 pesos as Commander in Chief of the army and it gives me the right to expect additional concessions and awards; and the law that declares the salaries of all public servants confers upon me as President of the Republic the salary of 50,000 pesos annually from the year 1819 on. I waive, from this moment on, all the rights and payments that I have not received, accepting in full payment for all of them the 14,000 pesos given to me in Bogotá."[68]

Three years later, at Pativilca, enfeebled by a serious illness and by exhaustion, he wrote again to the Congress of Colombia and, after presenting his resignation from the office of President of the Republic, in order to "protect my only treasure, my reputation," he said, "I immediately waive the pension of thirty thousand pesos annually which the munificence of the Congress has had the goodness to bestow upon me. I do not need it to live, and in the meantime the public treasury is exhausted."[69]

When the Peruvian Congress wanted to recompense him for his services with a million pesos, he refused the offer with dignity and not without a certain displeasure: "I note with infinite satisfaction," he said to the president of the Congress, "the determination to show me a recognition that, in truth, has already gone beyond ordinary bounds. As a consequence of these excessive demonstrations, I have come to be the beneficiary, and, on that account, a debtor in gratitude; but no matter how tenacious the Constituent Congress may be, my own tenacity cannot be exceeded, since there is no human power that can oblige me to accept a gift that my conscience refuses. I repeat to your excellency that, without accepting the award in question, my services are already recompensed infinitely more than I ever dared hope. Your excellency knows whether the Congress has left anything undone that would be pleasing to me . . . It has named me Father and Savior of Peru, it has decreed me the honor of Permanent President, it has ordered that my image be carved on a medal, it has called me Liberator, and it has required me to take charge of the government in Peru, and afterward sets aside for me an enormous fortune. I have accepted everything joyfully, except for the last, because the laws of my country and those of my heart prohibit it."[70]

During the whole of the war of independence Bolívar drew on his own funds for his living expenses, to help his friends, and to defray some of the expenses of the campaigns. When the resources of the treasury allowed, the salaries of those under his command were paid from that source, but those resources were generally insufficient to sustain the officers and friends who came running to him. His letters to his sister María Antonia, to whom he had assigned power of attorney, are numerous—requesting money, ordering payments and grants—for he believed that the public treasury ought not be made to serve to give satisfaction to the generosity of his own heart.

Few are the men of equal disinterest. He was born rich and he died in the most miserable poverty, while other men, some with genuine merits and services, enriched themselves during the performance of public duties, not only in Venezuela and New Granada, but in the whole of America. In contrast, Bolívar never used government money to provide benefits to himself personally. He even refused to use his influence in the defense of his own financial interests. The influence peddler, who has furnished unscrupulous governments with such notable revenues, was cast aside by the Liberator as unworthy of his noble hierarchy and as a humiliation to the persons who might turn to him or utilize his services. To his sister María Antonia, who suggested that he intervene with a judge in Caracas in order to achieve a prompt and satisfactory resolution of a legal matter in his interest, he answered, visibly offended, "I will not write to any judge about the Lecumberri lawsuit, no matter how much you insist. I do not wish to exceed the limits of my rights, which, to the degree that my position is elevated, are more restricted. Fate has placed me at the height of power, but I do not wish to have any other rights than those of the most simple citizen. Let justice be done, and let it be in my favor if it is on my side. If it is not on my side, I will receive the judgment of the court with tranquillity. Don't be anxious, however, for my titles are the best."[71]

That justice be done for others and for himself was his highest aspiration, because the rights of power neither annul nor diminish the rights of the rulers. A beautiful lesson in restricting dominion within the limits laid down by the law, which many rulers

do not know how to respect. In order to preserve their judiciousness, they ought to cover their ears so as not to succumb to the
ingratiations and the most self-seeking flattery that try to get
them to stray from the law and begin to hustle along the short
cuts that lead to worthlessness and lower the majesty of public
service.

The teaching of Bolívar to his sister extends to an entire people, to America as a whole, where most people, and above all
the rulers of elastic justice, try to cut the law to their own measure when the defense of their prerogatives is at stake, but give
it a narrow opening, a funnel with an ignominious passage,
when it is required to open a channel to the rights of the people,
to the just aspirations of the humble and dispossessed. From
Bolívar they must learn that at the summit of power rights are
reduced because the weight of duties falls there. Those rights
ought not be greater, but neither should they be lesser, than
those of the simple citizen when it is time for doing justice to
all.

I have presented Bolívar in one aspect, his pedagogical action,
in his guiding and shaping attitude, which is how I understand
him and how I would like him to be seen by the young, by
the teachers, by all the peoples of America. It is my conviction,
as I have said before, that what is truly formative for the personality of a people, who are a multiple student, and for the
individual student, is the exemplary, living, and active personality of the teacher, in his works, in what he says, and in what
he suggests, moving among difficulties and overcoming them.
From ancient times Plutarch had a sense of the value of biography for this formative necessity and he wrote his *Parallel Lives*.
In Bolívar we Americans have a perennial educational force, a
clear and exemplary life, full of ideals, of efforts, of sacrifices,
and it must help us because, as he himself said, "while there is
still something to be done, nothing has as yet been done." And
in America there are many things to be done.

Part Two

BOLÍVAR ON THE POLITICS
OF EDUCATION

1. GENERAL IDEAS

As we have seen, the life of Bolívar serves as a model, and this is the guiding function of all great teachers, who teach more by what they do than by what they say. However, in Bolívar we may also go in search of a pedagogical thought that governs his educational activity. His original ideas constitute an adequate orientation through which to achieve, along with the educational transformation that was necessary following the rupture with the old order, the economic independence and the social and cultural improvements demanded by the new order.

Bolívar, as a statesman, foresaw the transforming function of education, without which neither the liberty of the people nor the independence of the nation could be firmly established. To educate is also a political function, implicit in all the work of the government; and the statesman, who exercises a guiding role in fixing the political directions of the state, determines behavior, corrects vices, and assumes the supreme task of making the law into a path of improvement and a frame to contain the excessive ambitions of some in the face of the necessities and the just aspirations of others.

The educational thought of Bolívar runs through his letters, speeches, and public documents. Some people find in that thought traces of Rousseau and of other thinkers of the time, which is not strange, because the representative men of a historical period have a frame of reference within which they express the concerns of the moment. The original personality takes from that frame in order to return to it, now enriched with his own personal contributions, the concepts which serve to make him understood by his contemporaries. Only he who speaks the language of his times can make himself understood by his fellow men. Those who command and direct, if they wish to be heard and followed, have to express themselves through ideas that, since they make up part of the substratum of everybody's consciousness, achieve resonances in the minds of all.

Rousseau filled a whole historical stage. His thought oriented

the men of the French Revolution. Kant praised him, Goethe
followed him, Pestalozzi applied him, and even Diderot, who
sometimes criticized him, admitted him along with D'Alembert
among the editors of the Encyclopedia. Even today, the advo-
cates of the so-called active school or child-centered school find
in Rousseau their most characteristic inspiration, in spite of the
two centuries that have passed since the publication of his *Emile*.
However, Rousseau was a philosopher and Bolívar was a politician, a statesman. The former thought of education as an idea,
the latter conceived it as an indispensable instrument in the task
of effective management of the state. For that reason, in most
instances the thought of Bolívar and that of Rousseau do not
coincide but, on the contrary, contradict or exclude one another.

The Genevan planned the education of Emile in contact with
nature in order to take him away from the noxious influence of
society. His student, belonging to the upper class, was able to
pay for education with a farseeing tutor. For Bolívar the problem was to educate a whole people, and for that reason he made
public education compulsory in Colombia, Peru, and Bolivia and
put it under the care of the state, since it is to the state, according
to his ideas, that the creation and direction of education pertain. On this doctrine he was sufficiently explicit in the speech
at Angostura and in the proposal for a Commission on Education, which was a part of his proposed fourth branch of government, the moral branch. He said, "Establishing, organizing, and
directing primary schools, for boys as well as for girls, belongs
exclusively to the Commission."[72]

The idea of compulsory public education, above all that it be
compulsory, was not accepted by the liberal spirit of some of
the members of the Assembly of the French Revolution. Condorcet, Talleyrand, Mirabeau, and others spoke against it, although it was brilliantly defended by Robespierre.

His lack of confidence in the society of his time led Rousseau
to oppose public education, in spite of his having agreed, in his
article on political economy in 1753, nine years before the publication of *Emile*, that "public education, under the control of
regulations imposed by the government and of orders of magistrates named by the sovereign, is one of the fundamental
principles of popular and legitimate government."[73] And in his
work on the government of Poland, in 1772, ten years *after* the

publication of *Emile*, he stated, "It is education that ought to give to souls the national form and to direct their opinions and their likings in such a way that they will be patriotic by inclination, by passion, and by necessity." And farther on, "The law must regulate the contents, the sequence, and the methods of education."[74] But Rousseau believed that his ideas on public education, which according to him existed in a limited way among three peoples of antiquity, cannot now be realized on account of social corruption. In *Emile* he said, "Today public institutions do not and cannot exist, because where there is no country there is no citizen." And he added, "I do not take for institutions of public education those laughable establishments people call schools."[75]

For Rousseau *public education presupposes a society of free men;* for Bolívar *freedom is created by way of education.*

Bolívar could have derived his ideas on compulsory public education from the men who discussed this subject in revolutionary France or who came from Germany, where the Reformation had put it into practice from the sixteenth century on.

It is a matter of fact that the men of the French Revolution were opposed to the household system of education then prevailing in the nation. The deputy Ducos, in the Assembly session on December 18, 1792, discussing the establishment of primary education common for all citizens, which had been proposed in the Lanthenas report, stated, "I believe that all the children born in the Republic, whatever the social condition or the wealth of their parents, ought to be educated so that later on they may become public employees required to serve for a definite period of time in public primary schools. That requirement, it will be exclaimed, would be too much and too forcibly opposed to our habits and customs! And I reply that it is precisely for that reason that I propose it. The customs of a corrupt people will not be regenerated with soft sweetnesses, but with vigorous and brusque institutions. We have to choose openly between education in the household and liberty. Because, citizens, until through giving them a common education you have brought the rich nearer to the poor, the weak nearer to the powerful, until—to express myself in the words of Plutarch—you have directed along the same track and shaped within the same model of virtue all the children of the fatherland, it will be in vain that your laws promulgate equality. The Republic will remain divided into two classes: the *citizens* and the *masters*." In that same session the deputy J. B. Leclerc said, "What is it that is necessary, then, in order to regenerate our customs? A common education. We will never achieve anything except by this means. It has to be decreed that nobody will be exempt from the necessity of sending their children to the school of the citizen."[76]

However, it might be supposed that the concept of the public school maintained by Bolívar was derived from Quintilian, the ancient rhetorician, since Bolívar himself says in a work on "Public Education," written in 1825, "Quintilian prefers public schools to private instruction, because, in addition to the advantages afforded by the contact and conversation with people of different talents, here, he says, is where true friendships are made, those that last the whole of one's life."[77] But the public school in the form in which Bolívar thought of it was unknown to the Romans, since what we are concerned with here is an institution born out of the Reformation. What Quintilian called a public school should rather be called a school open to the public, in contrast with the schooling conducted at home. Such a school open to the public was opened by a teacher who received several students who paid him for the instruction he gave. This is what today we know as a private school (but which in Great Britain, in the Quintilian tradition, is still called a "public" school), in which in ancient times the state had no role and in which there was no form of public regulation, except in matters referring to morality, which in Rome were regulated even in private life.[78]

But the important thing is to emphasize that the compulsory character of public education as Bolívar conceived it serves the purpose of securing freedom and eliminating the effects of tyranny and slavery. He had said, in fact, "There can be no liberty where there is ignorance. Slavery is the child of darkness. An ignorant people is the blind instrument of its own destruction."[79] His experience had shown him that the cause of freedom, which he was struggling for, was not understood by everybody as the supreme good. The very slaves who were freed continued under the yoke of their old masters and followed them to other lands to which they had fled. Bolívar argued in the speech at Angostura that "ignorant people are more easily deceived than nature perfected by education." In that statement he was undoubtedly remembering Diderot, for whom "it is more difficult to oppress a peasant who knows how to read and write than it is an ignorant one."[80] However, it is not only of ignorance among the common people that Bolívar was speaking. Many of his lieutenants adopted torturous courses of action that not a few times threatened the outcome of the task of emancipation. "Treason and servility," Blanco-Fombona considered their attitude.[81] What is certain is that generous ideas are not comprehended in all their profundity except by lucid minds and by cultivated spirits, free from prejudice and restricting mental habits. Passage for great truths is opened up within the density of centuries only after education has shed light upon them, and, more than education, culture, taken in its strict sense, culture which elucidates, clarifies, and refines consciousness and puts into circulation new ways of interpreting and understanding the world. The Liberator himself justifies that behavior of his fellow citizens, at times inexplicable. "The contagion of despotism," he says, "has impregnated our atmosphere, and not even the fires of warfare nor the specific remedy of our health-giving laws have purified the air we breathe. Our hands are free, and yet our hearts suffer the chronic ills of servitude."[82]

After liberating the shackled hands and putting an end to physical and political servitude, it was necessary to liberate the spirits of men from moral servitude, from the spiritual burden, and from a situation of submission that diminishes men and makes them into victims even of what they detest, converting them into "born enemies of their own existence."

In order to provide a secure basis for his demands for a government-supported system of education, Bolívar reasoned in Angostura, "Bound under the triple yoke of ignorance, tyranny, and vice, the American people have not been able to acquire knowledge, power, or virtue. We have been students of such depraved teachers that the lessons we have received and the models we have studied are the most destructive. We have been dominated more by means of deceit than by force, and we have been degraded by vice more than by superstition." And he continued, "Ambition and intrigue abuse the credulity and the lack of experience of men to whom all political, economic, and social knowledge is alien, adopt as realities what are absolute illusions, take license for liberty, treason for patriotism, vengeance for justice; similar to the robust blind man who, incited by the sense of his own strength, sets off with the sureness of the most keensighted man and, falling into every snare, is unable to mend his ways."[83]

In the face of the need to reform the society to which freedom had recently dawned, the statesman strove for a path certain to lead to advancement. He sought inspiration in the men of the Encyclopedia and in the men of the French Revolution, whose works had been the main sustenance of his reading in Europe, in whom he found a blind faith in the power of education.[84] Perhaps he was to remember that, for Talleyrand, "for there to be liberty, education is necessary"; that, according to Turgot, "education has as its function the training of citizens"; and, above all, he might have invoked Montesquieu, who said, "The republican regime is that which needs all the effectiveness of education. The fear in which despotic governments are held is born spontaneously out of threats and punishments; honor in monarchies is fostered by the passions, which are in turn fostered by it; but political virtue is abnegation, unselfishness, the most difficult thing there is." Montesquieu also said, "This virtue may be defined by saying that it is the love of country and of its laws. This love, which always prefers the public good, engenders all private virtues, which consist in that preference."[85]

From that Bolívar was to declare in Angostura, "Popular education ought to be the first concern of the paternal love expressed by this Congress. Morality and enlightenment are the two poles of a Republic; morality and enlightenment are our first necessities." Because, for Bolívar, "the progress of enlightenment is that which advances the progress of custom, and uprightness of spirit is what advances the progress of enlightenment."[86] The thought of the Enlightenment guided him in that search for a path of moral regeneration and for the creation of a new spirit capable of the orderly enjoyment of the conquered freedom. The practice of virtue within the rule of law is for Bolívar a secure path. Training citizens to be just is one of his preoccupations because, in his thought, "good customs and not force are the tablets of the law, for the army of justice is the army of freedom."[87]

In a letter to Jeremy Bentham, sent from Caracas on January 15, 1827, reaffirming that idea about the power of enlightenment and of science in general to conquer and support liberty, Bolívar argued, "Unfortunately the weight of slavery extinguishes the spirit and places it in a condition in which it becomes unworthy of freedom. But that is the reason why the cultivation of the sciences, of which you speak to me, merits so much attention, so that man, even in the midst of his chains, may be enabled to discover, perhaps, that he possesses rights which must be defended."[88]

This faith in science marks a disagreement with Rousseau, who, as is well known, was the partisan of a negative education, opposed to the use of books, since they function as a screen upon the senses, which are the only instrument for the penetration of nature. Rousseau does not admit an existing science which Emile learns, but a science discovered, or rather rediscovered, through the application of the senses in a constant experiencing of natural phenomena. Rousseau protested against scientific artifacts, in order to appeal to "necessity" and to the freedom to make use of it without restriction.

2. THE QUALITIES OF THE LEADER

Bolívar possessed a fine educational intuition, which he brought into play on all those occasions in which leadership was required. His will to influence others in order to bring about behavior adequate to popular interests and national aspirations inspired in him ideas of his own about the work of the teacher, because in the genuine statesman, in the true leader, the pedagogical attitude is of the very essence of his will to command.

In the authentic educator and in the effective leader four fundamental characteristics come together:

    a. Confidence in education as a force for the transformation of human life and as an instrument for the alteration of social structures.

    b. Faith in the future, toward which educational work is projected.

    c. Confidence in educational possibilities, in the possibility of changes in the being who receives education and in the society in which it functions.

d. Creative capacity and ability to bring into the service of educative tasks the full range of material and spiritual resources.

Bolívar possessed these four qualities to the highest degree, and they were expressed as much in his activities as in his writings. All his work is a faithful image and expression of those qualities of the leader.

Confidence in the power of education. Confidence in education gives life to educational purposes. The eighteenth century, reacting against the thesis of original sin, which condemned man to the burden of an inheritance of evil from which he was not able to redeem himself except through the process of grace, gave urgent life to this faith in the work of education. Helvétius said, "Education can do everything." And, "Study is the whole of man."[89] It is true that already in the seventeenth century Leibniz had said, "Give me control over education for a few years, and I will take on the task of transforming the world." And for Comenius, also writing in the seventeenth century, only education allows the passage from animality to humanity. The Czech educator explained that man is a "trainable animal" and that "a man really cannot in any way educate himself without submitting to discipline."[90]

Bolívar, heir to this optimistic intellectual tradition of the seventeenth century and of the Encyclopedia, of the "century of Enlightenment," also believed in the unlimited power of education. Human conduct is capable of being perfected; progress finds a ready and unlimited path in education. There is neither happiness nor a secure future without education. For all these reasons, speaking as a statesman, in an article written in 1825, he places his faith in education. He asserts there, "The government shapes the morals of the people, it puts them on the road to greatness, to prosperity, to power. Why? Because, having charge of the elements of society, it establishes public education and directs it. The nation will be wise, virtuous, soldierly, if the principles of its education are wise, virtuous, and military; it will be foolish, superstitious, effeminate, and fanatic, if it is nursed in the school of these errors. That is why illustrious societies have always placed public education among the bases of its political institutions." After citing the examples of the republics of Plato, of Athens, Sparta, Rome, and the United States, which have put into practice positive principles in the orientation of education, he concludes, "Nations march toward the achievement of their greatness at the same pace with which education advances. They fly if this flies, go backward if it goes backward, fall and sink into obscurity if it is corrupted or completely abandoned. These principles, dictated by experience and inculcated by philosophers and politicians, both ancient and modern, today compose a doctrine so well known that perhaps hardly a single individual is to be found who does not feel himself profoundly affected by its truth."[91]

To his sister María Antonia, in order to emphasize to her the necessity of giving a careful education to his nephew Fernando, he wrote, "A man without studies is an incomplete being. Instruction is the happiness of life; and the ignorant person, who is always on the verge to returning to the mud of corruption itself, will soon fall inexorably into the darkness of servitude."[92]

This faith in education guided his labors as a leader and gave direction to multiple tasks, among which is his conern with establishing schools in Venezuela, in New Granada, in Ecuador, in Peru, in Bolivia, where he placed Simón Rodríguez, his own teacher, in charge of the administration of education.

Faith in the future. The task of independence, assumed by Bolívar, expresses not only the purpose of cutting the bonds of America's submission to the Spanish Empire, but that of projecting the consequences of a state of liberty into future time and through distant space. The dream of a free America complemented the dream of a free and better humanity; incorporating America, through what it represents, into the concert of nations, each sovereign of its own destiny.

The future of America was the hinge and guide of his liberating activity. In the "Jamaican Letter" of 1815, he pointed out, "I desire more than any other thing to see taking shape in America the greatest nation on earth, but a nation great less on account of its vastness and its riches than for its liberty and its glory." In that same letter he had said previously, in order to show his confidence in the final outcome of the struggle, "Success will crown our efforts, because the destiny of America has been irrevocably determined."[93]

At another time he says, "My hope in America grows stronger every day. America is not a problem, not even a fact: it is a sovereign decree of destiny, and irrevocable. This world cannot be bound to anything. Two great oceans surround it, and at heart the Americans are absolutely independent."[94]

But faith alone was not enough to raise hardly liberated peoples to the status of nations. The Americans of the South—a mixture of races, who even in Spain had mingled their bloodstreams, united later to the autocthonous Indian and to the contingent of African blood in the inhospitable environment of a wild, not yet conquered nature—would require a continuous process of unification, of purification, of improvement, and this was expressed in the purpose of ordering the chaos of the newly born republics, bringing into play all the moral faculties, all authority "in order to fuse the mass of people into a whole, the composition of the government into a whole, the legislature into a whole, the national spirit into a whole." And then Bolívar proclaims, *"Unity, unity, unity*—this must be our slogan."[95] He aspired toward unity in a place where everything conspired against it, because without cultural unity, which is the touchstone of social and political organization, no constitution prospers. For this reason Bolívar appeals to education as the basis of moral progress, as the guarantor of the future. The fourth branch of government proposed by him as a pillar of the republic was to be a center of moral and cultural sustenance. "Meditating," he said, "on the most effective way of regenerating the character and the customs that the tyranny and the war have left us with, I experienced the audacity of inventing a moral power, drawn from the depths of dark antiquity and from those forgotten laws that for a time maintained virtue among the Greeks and Romans."[96]

Concerned with public morals, which are the foundation of a democratic republic, he asked of the Legislature, "Let us create this Areopagus so that it will watch over the education of children, over national instruction; so that it may purify whatever there might be of corruption in the Republic; so that it may denounce ingratitude, selfishness, indifference toward love of country, idleness, the negligence of citizens; so that it may judge the beginnings of corruption, of pernicious models, being obliged to correct the customs of the people with moral punishments, just as the laws penalize crimes with physical punishments, and not only what collides with them but whatever weakens them, not only what violates the constitution but what violates public opinion."[97] The jurisdiction of this truly saintly tribunal would have to extend over education and instruction.[98]

Bolívar believed that the occupation of legislating requires special preparation. He conceived a hereditary senate made up of the liberators and their descendants, who were to be educated for their functions in a special school. The leaders of the republic should be carefully chosen and receive careful education, and if it was outlandish to propose hereditary senators in a democratic nation, the suggestion that whoever assumes public functions must have special training in order to exercise these functions finds its justification in the present concern with preparing leaders and with training them in how to lead and direct others. Heredity, to be sure, is no guarantee of ability; but the opportunity of educating the best people, without taking into account their origin or condition, will make sure that service is placed in the hands of those who have adequate training for the performance of this service.

This was a conservative idea, this idea of a hereditary senate, with senators educated for their calling in a special college, where they would learn "the arts, the sciences, and the letters that adorn the spirit of the public man." It was conservative as much on account of the exclusive designation of a class of men to a public profession as it was by virtue of the specialization of their education, which was undoubtedly to be forbidden to other citizens. But it has to be understood and judged in relation to its intended objective. Bolívar had previously observed in the "Jamaican Letter" that there was a grievous lack of persons capable of serving the republic. He stated, "The Americans have risen suddenly and without preparatory knowledge and, what is more relevant, without practice in the performance of public duties, to act out on the stage of the world the eminent roles of legislators, magistrates, administrators of public finances, diplomats, generals, and all other such supreme authorities and subordinates as make up the hierarchy of a regularly constituted state."[99] In addition, while many were thinking in terms of a throne raised over the American lands, with a hereditary nobility,

Bolívar's idea tended toward the preservation of the democratic republic while conceding to the partisans of the monarchy a formula that would accommodate their ambitions. That idea was made more palpable in the proposed Constitution of Bolivia, in which Bolívar proposed a presidency and a Chamber of Censors whose terms of office would be for life. This was presented in the form of a reply to those who upheld Napoleonic ideas and suggested to Bolívar that he crown himself Emperor. In a letter to General Pedro Briceño Méndez, after rejecting the proposal of José Antonio Páez and his friends that he crown himself, he said, "After the most considered meditations I have come to believe that the best remedy we are able to apply to an evil that could be fatal to us is that I send to Páez my proposal for a Constitution for Bolivia in answer to the letter he has written to me and with the objective that he come to understand my ideas about stability united with liberty and the preservation of the principles we have adopted."[100] He tried to give a masterful lesson in judiciousness.

The conservatism of the educator is implicit in the very process of his work, which is in part renovation and creation but which clings to the roots of a culture that grows more fruitful as it takes possession of the subsoil of traditions that nourish it. Every creator is an innovator and a preserver at the same time, and Bolívar, creator and teacher of his people, was not able to escape from this principle. The creator, if he loves his work and is convinced of its importance, tends to conserve it, with the aim of making participants in its values out of those who, without the capacity to invent beneficial things, are able to waste or to destroy the good things they already possess. And the work of Bolívar was the freedom of America, the creation of republics on half a continent, and within them the founding of a democratic way of life with civil and political equality. In the face of those who opposed that work, in the face of the reckless people who demanded reforms even before the achieved conquests had been secured, and against those who wanted to go backward, Bolívar established an equilibrium, thereby giving a lesson in optimism and of faith in America and its free institutions. According to him, educated America would break the trail along which future generations would improve themselves with every passing day. His educational fervor led him to state, "I have brought about the establishment of a liberal system in the whole of Colombia and that alone will make the coming generation very much superior to the present one."[101]

Confidence in educational possibilities. Rousseau believed that man was born good and that society made him evil. For the Genevan the education of Emile was to be realized in contact with nature, far from that society in which the perversion of customs would impede the sound education of the spirit. Bolívar did not believe in any such original innate goodness of man, but he did presuppose his redemption. As Blanco-Fombona stated, Bolívar believed that "man can raise himself above himself by the power of examples and through education."[102]

Bolívar provided a continuing series of exemplary deeds in his own conduct, and his constant preoccupation echoed *this* regenerative purpose—the formation of a democratic consciousness for the scrupulous exercise of freedom. To Guillermo White, who had formulated severe criticisms of his idea of hereditary senators, he wrote, "Education will create the moral man, the man of justice, and the man of law." In that same letter he asserted, "I have very little trust in the morality of our fellow citizens, and without republican morality there cannot be a free government. In order to secure this morality, I have invented a fourth power that would bring men up in virtue and maintain them in it." That faith in education implied also the trust that education would respond to the incentives that were to be given it, and thus, like Rousseau, who, though he was no partisan of punishment, had said that "one ought to employ force with children and reason with men," the Liberator believed that even with men violence was necessary in order to make them accept the beneficial norms intended to improve their human condition and their social life. "If there is any just violence," he said, "it is that which is employed to make men good, and consequently, happy; and there is no legitimate liberty except where this is directed toward honoring humanity and perfecting its fate."[103]

Creative capacity. Bolívar's creative capacity as a great leader of peoples was demonstrated in the ways conceived by him to make it possible that, along with the conquered freedom, the morality necessary to preserve the independence of the republic should be secured among the people.

As we have seen, in America tyranny assumed all its habitual forms of public immorality, since slavery had engendered attitudes of indulgence and immorality that compromised, not only the acceptance of the recently created juridical institutions, but the efficacy of the laws established for the purposes of achieving equality and the security of life in citizenship. Therefore, along with the traditional structures of the state proposed by Locke and Montesquieu and with the accustomed forms laid down in the political charters of the United States, of France, and of Great Britain, which served him as a model, Bolívar created new structures, in which he placed side by side with the specific value of juridical norms, which in their functioning and evaluative essence add up to the exercise of sanctions, the moral norm, which has its basis in conscience and attains its realization in the general concensus of the community.

In the draft for a constitution which he presented to the Congress at Angostura, Bolívar conceived a Moral Power, to which reference has already been made and which will be looked at from the juridical point of view in the next section of this essay. Here we would like to analyze this conception in its educational and ethical aspects, since, above all, this proposed institution was to have been, as its name indicates, an organization for public morality.

Bolívar created nations and established the regime of liberty in the nations newly born to political independence. "A potter of republics," he called himself in a letter to Santander in May of 1824, "a trade," he said, "of no little hard work, but at the same time glorious."[104] This potter's art of republics placed unformed clay in the hands of the artificer, so that into the vessel might flow the content of his people, which like water takes on the form of the vase that holds it; and this is the educational mission of institutions, of laws, which serve in society as molds for the peaceful passage of the soul of the citizenry.

In men accustomed to living under the secular yoke of a foreign power, Bolívar set about creating the consciousness that they were masters of their own destiny and that they had passed from the condition of slavery to the noble quality of citizenship. Such consciousness is not to be formed except through the prolonged exercise of liberty, because only in that atmosphere do men live freely and work together for the preservation of the order that sustains them, in whose norms the purpose of progress and social stability is implicit.

America came out of chaos, out of social and political chaos. Bolívar had said in the "Jamaican Letter" in 1815, "We are a small mankind. We have an open world surrounded by extensive seas, new in almost all the arts and sciences, although in certain ways old in the usages of civil society." He said then that we were similar to the peoples who were isolated at the fall of the Roman Empire, each one of whom formed its own government to the measure of its chiefs or of the family or guilds with sufficient influence. However, those nations returned to the customary ways of their secular traditions. "But we, who hardly preserve even any vestiges of what existed in former times, and who, on the other hand, are neither Indians nor Europeans but a type halfway between the legitimate owners of the country and the Spanish Europeans,"[105] require special treatment and an organization adequate to contain the ambitions of some, the caste dominance of others, and, above all, the desire to maintain privileges that lead to the deterioration of the majority of the people, in whose favor independence had been gained.

Bolívar sought a kind of political organization for the peoples freed by him that, while adjusting itself to the principles expressed by Montesquieu, would conform more to existing necessities and to the aspirations and conditions of our countries than to a political theory. "The most perfect system of government," he concluded, "is that which produces the greatest amount of happiness possible, the greatest amount of social security, and the greatest amount of political stability." And in another place he maintained, "The excellence of a government does not consist in its theory, nor in its form nor in its mechanism, but in its being appropriate to the nature and character of the nation of which it is constituted."[106]

As the leader of his people, consubstantial with them, he sought not just any political form, but a constitution that would be at one and the same time a juridical organization and an interwoven system of public and private morals, and that would serve as a school for citizenship or as an epitome on good behavior in the republic.

Thinking of Lycurgus, author of the constitution of ancient Sparta, Bolívar sought a system of legislation that would shape creative virtue, shape morality, and would create national glory and happiness. He knew, however, that it is not laws but men and their example who constitute a republic—for, as he maintained, "virtuous men, patriotic men, illustrious men, constitute the Republic." That is why he took upon himself the task of drawing up the constitutional texts that he presented to the Congress of Angostura in 1819 and to the Constituent Assembly of the recently created Republic of Bolivia in 1826.

What interests us is to point out in these constitutional texts whatever is related to Bolívar's educational mission, to his pedagogical attitude. The other parts of these constitutions are framed within the political theory that was predominant at the time, and, for that reason, the analysis of them is more accessible and has been realized from several points of view. What we want to find in Bolívar is the prominent track of a spirit projected toward the future of our nationalities through the creation of ways of behaving and of attitudes leading toward the achievement of a regime of justice, by means of the propagation of a culture and of a system of popular education.

In the proposal for a constitution formulated by Bolívar for the Congress of Angostura, written in his own handwriting, he included as an integral part the stipulation for what he called Areopagus, or Moral Power.

Contrary opinions have been expressed about this Moral Power, which Bolívar tried to derive from the ancient institutions of Greece and Rome, giving it dominion "over childhood, over the hearts of men, over public opinion, good customs, and republican morals."[107]

Some of the opinions expressed about that creation of Bolívar's take note only of what is incongruent in the act of placing an ensemble of ethical norms, without possible enforcement and without sanction against those who violate them, within a juridical ordinance. However, in all the constitutions of the eighteenth and nineteenth centuries, moral principles are to be found mingled with juridical principles, and even in the constitutions of our own century numerous principles without possible sanction figure, due to the fact that what Mirkine Guetzevitch[108] calls "the principle of the rationalization of rights" has carried into the body of the constitution numerous moral precepts, simple recommendations that, in spite of their unenforceability, serve as incentives to struggle and as motives to the growth of the social process and of its organization.

If it be judged from the strictly juridical point of view, the Moral Power is without meaning and might be considered a useless appendage to the body of the Constitution. For us, however, the Moral Power is to be explained as the crystallization of a pedagogical theory, of an educational system, without which a systematic education could not be conceived, just as it is not possible to conceive revolution without revolutionary theory nor political organization without political theory.

Bolívar, the creator of nations, was obliged to conceive for these nations constitutional statutes in which aspirations and desires, ideals and purposes would find room and, above all, where liberty, justice, and equality, which were the motives in the name of which the Revolution for Independence had been made, would be realized. A pedagogical theory, however, cannot exist separate from a theory of the state, nor apart from a theory of society. The educator thinks in terms of the ideal man and in order to shape him takes values arranged in a scale of preferences that will convert him into the best. But such a man has to live within a society, he is the subject of rights, and then, of course, he lives with others within a nation; he is a citizen, in whom the purpose pursued by the Constitution of the state is made effective. Being a subject of law he is obliged to fulfill the duties imposed by the Constitution. As an educator, Bolívar believed in moral man, capable of doing justice and of asking it for others, a soldier of freedom, respectful of the law and loving toward his country— that is to say, the complete citizen.

3. THE COMMISSION ON MORALS

The moral branch of government, conceived by Bolívar as part of the Constitution in 1819 and rejected by the legislators at Angostura, has two divisions of unequal value, the Commission on Morals and the Commission on Education.

In my opinion, the Commission on Morals, in spite of its relation to Greek and Roman institutions, expresses Bolívar's intention to counterpose an organism of opinion to the all-powerful organism of central power in the unitary republic—which in the Constitution of Angostura was to have been substituted for the federal republic established by the first Congress of 1811. In effect, Article 4 of the second section of the part of the Constitution devoted to the moral branch of government makes clear that "its jurisdiction extends not only to individuals but to the family, to the provinces, to institutions, to the courts, to all authorities, and even to the Republic as a whole. If they come to be immoral, they ought to be denounced to the whole world. The government itself is subject to its jurisdiction, and it might place upon the government a mark of infamy and declare it unworthy of the Republic if it breaks treaties or misrepresents them, if it violates any agreement or fails to fulfill any obligation or promise."[109]

The authority of the Areopagus was placed above all other authority; and Bolívar, in his opposition to the federal organization of the state (which was, according to him, the most perfect political form of democracy but, while most admirable for its excellences, least applicable to Venezuelan reality), wished to install a strong central government, with a powerful state, not handicapped or encumbered when it came to the need for action in defense of the republic and its institutions. However, above that state and that powerful executive branch, he placed a counterweight or moral balance wheel in order to restrain its impulses and to maintain them within the orbit of its obligations and commitments. However, it is also to be noted that the proposed Constitution of Angostura had suppressed any reference to the supposed right of the people to resist or repel all unjust aggression of the government or of its functionaries, a right consecrated among the four natural and irrevocable rights in the second article of the French Declaration of the Rights of Man and of the Citizen of 1789. These rights are given there as "liberty, property, security, and *resistance to oppression*." (Emphasis L.B.P.)

That last right had been established in the Federal Constitution of Venezuela of 1811, although in a more moderate and thoughtful form, following the formula of Section 3 of the Virginia

Bill of Rights of 1776.[110] In Article 191 of that constitution it is said, "Governments have been constituted for common happiness, for the protection and security of the peoples who compose it, and not for the beneficent honor and special interest of any man, of any family, or of any class of men in particular who make up only a part of the community. The best of all governments will be that which would be most appropriate for producing the greatest amount of good and of happiness and which would be most secure against the dangers of maladministration; *and any time that it is recognized that a government is incapable of fulfilling these objectives or that it be opposed to them, the majority of the nation unquestionably has the inalienable and irrevocable right to abolish it, to change it, or to reform it in whatever manner it may judge most appropriate.*"[111] (Emphasis L.B.P.)

On the contrary, in the Constitution of Angostura of 1819 it is stated, "The people of Venezuela cannot exercise for themselves any attributions of sovereignty other than that of elections, nor can they place it in only a few hands. The sovereign power will be divided with regard to its exercise between Legislative, Executive, and Judicial Powers."[112] In addition, among the duties of the citizen the following was established (in Article 4): "The citizen must not adapt himself simply to not breaking the law. It is necessary that he be watchful, in addition, over the observance of the law and that he take all steps within his capacity to see that it is fulfilled, employing example, persuasion, and *declarations to the authorities if all other means should prove ineffective.*"[113] (Emphasis L.B.P.)

The juridical formulation of rights in the Venezuelan Constitution of 1819, which was a mixture of ancient and modern institutions, and which was inspired by the Napoleonic constitutions, in spite of the fact that it adopted English constitutional traditions as a model, for what it contains of republicanism, probably led the Liberator to seek in an organism of the nature of the Areopagus a counterweight to the arbitrariness of the government and a safeguard to the rights of the citizens, with the end in view that they not find themselves forced to use violence in order to secure justice on their own. In any case, the watchfulness of the Moral Power reaches as much into governmental violations of the rights of the citizen as it does into the abandonment by the citizens of their moral duties.

With greater perspective in judgment it is now believed that the idea of the Liberator, in his later conception of a Board of Censors in the Proposal for a Constitution for Bolivia, was to try to seek a way of entry for public opinion, which was forced to accept a rigid organization in which the executive power was all-powerful and able to overturn the guarantees of civil rights.[114] This Board of Censors was a diminished copy of the Moral Power included in the proposed Constitution of Angostura and was easier to assimilate since it did not have the implications of a court of public morality but the specific functions of what in contemporary political law is known as the *ombudsman*, although with a different structure and with a different orientation.

The surreptitious guarantee sought by the Liberator for the people's right of resistance to oppression—a right formally stated in the Declaration of Independence of the United States, in the Constitution of France, and in the 1811 Constitution of Venezuela —through the creation of a legal organism co-ordinate with the executive power and charged with preventing and judging the excesses of governmental agents, placed those projects within the norms of the political structure already admitted, from which the right of the people to resist oppression had been excluded, in so far as they were to resort to force,[115] but maintains the predominance of the lifelong rule of an all-powerful President, against whom, were there no other recourse, as Victor Andrés Belaúnde observes, every crisis would be resolved by a *coup d'état*. Taking his inspiration from Montesquieu, whom he paraphrased in the speech at Angostura in his references to the Areopagus and especially in the speech in which he presented the Proposal for a Constitution for Bolivia in his reference to the censors, the Liberator, having already proposed organizations that would control the people, was thinking of the possibility of an organization that would control the government. "They [the censors]," he had said, "will be public prosecutors against the government, in order to see to it that the Constitution and public contracts are religiously observed."[116] According to Montesquieu, a common vigilance contributes to the conservation of the purity of customs and the stability of the republic.[117]

The Areopagus really does seem to be Utopian, for it is true,

as Marius André stated, that its sanctions would not be restricted
to the moral sphere alone, since the disqualification pronounced
by that tribunal would render those against whom its pro-
nouncements were made unfit for the exercise of public duties
and, upon disqualifying the government and its institutions, it
would incapacitate them from realizing their functions. It might
further be said that such a tribunal would also be unworkable:
first, on account of the complicated mechanism of its organization; and, second, on account of the impossibility of securing in
its composition the quality of men that the text of the project
supposes, since, according to this text, what we are dealing with
is "an essentially blameless and saintly tribunal." As was said in
the Congress of Angostura, its functioning would have constituted
a fatal moral inquisition; but, more than this, on account of the
constant vigilance of some over others, bent on seeing everywhere
the mote in the other person's eye, it would have contributed to
disunity; it would have fomented distrust; and, to sum up, in
place of being a guardian of the tablets of constitutional law, it
would have been converted into a Cerberus of the conscience and
an unpopular monster, upon which everybody would look as a
danger to freedom and a threat of aggression against the inmost
being of each citizen. But was that in fact the purpose intended
by Bolívar? Not at all. He was proposing an intellectual creation
apart from the commendable adaptation to reality proposed by
Montesquieu. Further, if we take into consideration the opinion
of Dr. Salcedo Bastardo, it would have been "of transitory existence, because its own success would have brought about its progressive liquidation: to the degree that the population becomes
ethically more perfect, controls will become superfluous, and it
will no longer be necessary for the state to take care of virtue.
The ordinary organs of education in virtue will, however, continue to exist, but without giving to this subject the character of
an enforced obligation."[118]

Perhaps the Liberator let himself be carried away by the
ruminations of Montesquieu. Montesquieu, taking leave of the
practical sense that, according to him, ought to inspire the spirit
of the laws, proposed disinterring from Greek and Roman
antiquity institutions for the moralization of customs that could
not possibly be made to function in a modern state.

In the light of these Bolivarian juridical creations, which are

imperious forms for controlling and modifying behavior in order
to shape the moral conscience of the people, it has been maintained that Bolívar "is a moralist and, for that reason, pes-
simistic."[119] Such a characterization would place Bolívar in the
realm of the philosophers, when everybody knows that his
boundless action situates him in the world of the politicians, for
whom doing makes sense when it tends to resolve the problems
posed by a changing reality.

It is true that Bolívar, as I have said before, did not share
the ingenuous belief of Rousseau that men are born good, but
neither did he hold to theological formulas that suppose man to
be perverted by original sin from which he can be saved only by
grace, nor, as Hobbes supposed, that "man is a wolf to man." His
idea of man in society was more modest, because he saw man
as the subject of rights within the state that itself creates those
rights. Within that state the principle of culture treats all with
strict impartiality, and it is positive law that establishes the
sanctions against violations of that principle.

Man is neither good nor evil; he is man—which is the same
thing as saying that all possibilities exist in him. In him vices
and virtues are found mingled together; and the politician, the
statesman, and above all if that statesman finds himself placed
in the position of educator of his people, has the obligation of
seeking ways to bring the virtues to flowering and to subdue the
vices, to the end that by pursuing the virtues man will render
benefits to society without causing harm through the manifesta-
tion of the vices.

In that sense institutions perform a lofty educational function.
When Bolívar proposes institutions and laws, he designs them to
the measure of the people he knows, who are not composed of
angels, but of human beings, a mixture of several strains, the
Spaniard, the Indian, the Negro, all of them reinforced by a wild
environment, by centuries of lack of culture, and, above all, by
a regime that created habits of servility in some and in others
exalted the passion for dominance—just as Bolívar described
them in the speech before the Congress of Angostura that is so
frequently quoted.

It was not on account of pessimism that Bolívar preferred
severe and inflexible laws, nor was it for that reason that he
sought systems distinct from those reigning among other peoples,

but because his sense of political reality caused him to observe, along with Montesquieu, that laws, like suits and dresses, ought to be cut to the measure of the people who live within them.

In Bolívar the politician and the educator walked hand in hand, engaged in this process of adapting pedagogical activity to the measure of the student and to make it agree with social necessities. It is for this reason that he formulates laws in which the people may be enabled to see themselves reflected in their habits and customs, restricting themselves within the boundaries of duty or raising themselves up in order to reclaim their violated rights.

To be an educator, and Bolívar was an educator to the highest degree, is to be an optimist, because the work of education looks toward the future and is a seed in time. Only he who has faith in the work of shaping human beings is able to educate. Only he who knows how to hope is able to gather in the harvest of successes in the man who is educated—twenty years after leaving the classroom. Bolívar planted with faith in the future. If, then, at the end he believed he had plowed the sea, the blame is to be placed on a spirit beaten down by sickness and fatigue. Of his work as a legislator little remains to us; of his work as an educator we preserve the spirit, so that we may say, in the midst of our difficulties, that education will pave the road to our welfare and to our happiness.

4. THE COMMISSION ON EDUCATION

But if criticisms of this sort bear upon the Commission on Morals, they are not equally pertinent to the Commission on Education. At the time of its conception this latter commission represented not only a structure appropriate to the direction of public education but a structure designed to respond to the purpose pursued by Bolívar—that of making out of the education of the people an instrument adequate to the tasks of fomenting morality and of creating, along with the consciousness of nationality, an attitude of respect for the law.

A sign of Bolívar's capacity for creativity, the Commission on Education was designed for the purpose of placing the whole realm of material and spiritual resources at the service of the task of bringing culture to the people. Let us see what it is that is original in this idea and the expressions it was subsequently given.

It was during the Reformation in the sixteenth century that the movement toward public education first saw the light of day, and with that development the dominion exercised by the church over the management of education was interrupted. Martin Luther, however, still considered the schools to be auxiliaries of the church. Beginning in 1717, with Frederick William I and Frederick II, called the Great, state education was initiated, and this form of schooling, even though it was inspired by the desire to build up the Prussian state by means of education, was continued under Lutheran influence. It was decreed that education should be compulsory; however, the sense of public service, which is essential to the dissemination and acquisition of education, was lacking.

Johann Bernhard Basedow, who is most famous for his influences on elementary education, conceived the idea of a Patriotic Council, a kind of government council on education, charged with maintaining constant vigilance over and taking care of everything having to do with education and culture; thus he sketched the structure of an organization of control over these important functions.

Rousseau, in his work on the government of Poland in 1772, said, "Whatever the form given to public education, it would be a good thing to establish a college of commissioners of the first rank who would have control over the general administration and who would name, discharge, and change at will all the principals and directors of the schools who would themselves be candidates for the higher administrative level."[120]

Turgot supported this idea of Rousseau's when he declared in 1775 that "the first and most important of all institutions must be a Council to direct the nation's education, and to this Council the general orientation of all universities, colleges, and schools would be answerable according to a uniform principle and, above all, from a national and public point of view."[121] Thus the centralist aim in education that has been traditional in France was expressed.

In 1784, Jacques Henri Bernardin de Saint-Pierre proposed the creation of "a permanent board of public education," composed of distinguished men who would be entrusted with reforming teaching methods and "who would cause uniformity to be observed as much as possible in all the schools of the realm with respect to the practices that have been demonstrated to be the best." In support of this proposition, Bernardin de Saint-Pierre reasoned, "To provide a good education to all children is one of the most important functions of the government and one of the concerns most worthy of the attention of the leaders of the state."[122]

This idea of a central body directing education was taken up by the men of the French Revolution. Talleyrand proposed a Commission of Public Instruction to take charge of the management of education and suggested that this commission be composed of six commissioners, with six adjutant inspectors.

But it was Condorcet, in his famous proposal for a decree presented to the Assembly in 1793, who most clearly conceived this organ of educational direction, which he called the National Society of Sciences and Arts, a body that would be charged with naming a directorship for education. However, for Condorcet, partisan of unlimited freedom of instruction as he was, the directive organ for education would not have any dependence on the official administrative authorities of the state, for he feared that these authorities would try to impose their partisan ideas. To this effect he said, "No public power could have the authority, nor even the influence, to impede the development of new truths, the teaching of theories contrary to their particular politics or to their momentary interests."[123] The autonomous organization proposed by Condorcet was to be entrusted to the teachers making up the National Society of Sciences and Arts, and would be responsible solely to the Parliament. It was to appoint a board of directors for education and assign the task of appointing teachers to it. In defense of this arrangement, he declared, "since it is the first condition of all instruction that nothing but truths shall be taught, the establishments of the public power consecrated to that end must be as independent as possible of all political authority, and since, however, this independence cannot be absolute, it follows from the same principle that it is necessary to make those establishments dependent only on the Assembly of the Representatives of the people, because of all powers it is the least corruptible, the most difficult to be swayed by private interests, the most subject to the influence of the general opinion of educated men, and, above all, although all changes essentially emanate from it, it is, for that reason, the least hostile to the progress of culture, the least opposed to the improvements that this progress ought to bring."[124]

The liberalism of Condorcet led him to deny compulsion in education, in spite of the fact that he believed that "education is, for the public power, an obligation of justice . . . imposed by the common interest of the society, by that of all of humanity."

The ideas opposed to compulsory education advanced by Condorcet and others were combatted by Robespierre in the Convention, where other, more radical proposals were presented. The one that was most generally accepted was that of Joseph Lakanal, who in 1793 proposed a Central Commission on Education, to be charged with establishing a uniform method of teaching and with promulgating the regulations that would determine the duties of teachers and the regimen of discipline in the schools.

Bolívar, undoubtedly, was acquainted with these ideas, but the originality of the Commission on Education that he proposed to the Congress of Angostura rested on the fact that for the first time it was intended to place in the text of the Constitution, not only the authorization of the right to education as a popular guarantee, as had been done in France in the Declaration of the Rights of Man and of the Citizen and in some of the state constitutions of the United States, but, in order to guarantee its fulfillment, the provision for an organization capable of directing it.

5. COMPULSORY EDUCATION AND THE EDUCATION OF MOTHERS

There is really no question here of an idea similar to that of Condorcet, since Bolívar thought of the education of the citizen not only as an obligation of the state, which it was obliged to offer its citizens, but as a right of the society, which it could require its citizens to accept. For that reason, he designated as the first responsibility of the Commission on Education that of directing the moral and physical education of children from birth to the age of twelve. Thus the issue here was compulsory education—of which the state would have charge and which would be under the control and orientation of the state.

Bolívar was approaching, from a legal point of view, the modern conception according to which the child is a being in the process of growth and according to which its education ought to be oriented by the state from the time of its birth.

Rousseau thought that "the education of a man begins when he is born; before he speaks and before he hears, he is instructed." Napoleon, who was not an educator, but a politician, maintained that "education begins twenty years before the birth of the child," that is, with the birth of the parents, who ought to be educated in order to be enabled, in their turn, to educate and direct their children.

This idea led Bolívar, first of all, to the Commission on Education, admirable as a juridical principle, when in Article 2 of his plan he said, "Since the co-operation of mothers is absolutely indispensable in the education of their children in the early years, and since these years are the most precious for the inculcation of fundamental ideas and the most imperiled on account of the delicacy of their organs, the Commission will take care very especially to publish and to disseminate among the people throughout the Republic definite brief and simple instructions, accommodated to the intelligence of all the mothers of families, upon one and another subject." This education was conceived to be obligatory in that mothers were to be required to take an examination on the knowledge they had acquired "on the day of baptism or when registering the birth of the child."[125]

Talleyrand, among others, fixed the upper age limit for compulsory primary education at twelve years, and this was fulfilled in the world many years later, being carried up to fourteen or fifteen years in some countries and, recently, up to sixteen or eighteen years in others, but including in these years schooling beyond the primary grades.

Rousseau, in spite of his having been, as we have seen, concerned for public or national education according to regulations prescribed by the government in his *Discourses on Political Economy* and in his *Considerations on the Government of Poland,* when he came to write *Emile* did not show himself to be a partisan of public education. At any rate he kept Emile, until he was twelve years old, under a regimen in which nature was his only teacher. The negative education that he was in favor of was a direct condemnation of everything created by society through judging it artificial.

However, he did take the care of mothers very much into account, and he declared himself against the use of hired wet nurses because, for him, without mothers children did not exist. He said, "Do you wish to make everybody abide by their primary duties? Begin with the mothers. You will be astonished at the changes produced in this way." This, of course, is not an idea of Rousseau's, but one that is consubstantial with the process of bringing up that is implicit in the meaning of the word *educate*.[126]

For Comenius, predecessor of Rousseau, the first step in instruction is the maternal school, *materni-gremi,* or school at the breast of the mother, where the mother is the first teacher. This school ought to last until the age of six, during which time the child is to receive from the mother the lessons that later on would be carried much deeper in the primary school. According to Comenius, "there ought to be a maternal school in every family, an elementary school in each community, a high school in each city, a college in each nation or even in each important province."[127]

The realization of a maternal school in each family, as Comenius proposed, would require the prior education of the mothers for the complete fulfillment of their educative functions, in the way that Bolívar proposed later.

It was Pestalozzi who tried to institutionalize maternal education by placing the education of the people in the hands of the mothers, when he created the theory of "the home as a classroom" in his works *Leonard and Gertrude* and *How Gertrude Teaches Her Children.* But that institution is a natural one, and Bolívar takes hold of it at the original root in the home in order to carry to it the fountains of knowledge, with the aim that the spirit of the citizens breathed into them by the mothers should grow out from the home.

Later, with Froebel, the creation of the kindergarten was

realized in Germany, and in France nursery schools were created, institutions quite widespread today throughout the world, as one consequence of the extraordinary consideration accorded the child. Bolívar anticipated this idea and raised it to the character of a fundamental educational concern, since, as we have seen, he conceived it as an obligation of all mothers, and this is a usage that is not yet achieved in any country, for in some countries the irreplaceable maternal function is assumed by institutions of the state.

This idea of the institutionalization of the home as a school, popularized by Pestalozzi, was expressed by Bolívar in Article 10 of the Commission on Education, which states, "Each school will be under the immediate supervision of a principal who will be appointed by the Commission, choosing him from among the most virtuous and learned men, regardless of the place of his birth. The wife of the principal will be the immediate governess of the girls, and those who fill these posts will be honored, respected, and loved as the first and most precious citizens of the Republic."[128]

Perhaps it could have been said that in a country of illiterates, where the education of women did not exist even in embryo and where that of men was deficient, the education of mothers through the passing out of instructional pamphlets would have been an impractical measure. But to make this criticism would have been, at the same time, to point out that for the Liberator the general education of men and women was essential for the protection of children and for their early care, for the promotion of public and private morality, and for the progress of institutions.

Bolívar's subsequent activities brought him to formalize a system of compulsory education—compulsory not only for citizens who were to receive it, but for the state that was to be responsible for it—when, by decree on December 11, 1825, he ordered in Bolivia "that the first obligation of the government is to give education to the people, uniform and general, and administered in establishments organized in accordance with the law," because "the salvation of the Republic depends upon the morals that the citizens acquire in their childhood through education."

In Article 4 of that same decree it was established, "That in the meantime and without loss of time, in each city that is the capital of a township, a primary school be established, with the divisions that belong to it in order to receive all the children of both sexes who are of school age." In December 1826, he widened the legal provisions of 1821 and 1826 on education in Colombia, which established the obligation for parents to "place their children in school and maintain them there until they learn to read and write."[129]

6. THE EDUCATIONAL IMPORTANCE OF BOOKS

There is nothing more anti-Rousseau than the idea of educating by means of books.

For Rousseau, "the child who reads does not think; he does nothing but read; he does not educate himself, he only learns words." In another place he says, "I hate books, because they only teach how to talk about what one does not know."[130]

In contradiction to this attitude, the men of the French Revolution devoted a great deal of attention to books for elementary instruction, and, to promote the production of them, the Convention held several contests. The historian of education Gabriel Campayre observes, "One of the happiest ideas of that time was that of wishing to place in the hands of parents simple methods, well-made books that would teach them how to educate their children."[131] Indeed, in the final days of the year 1792, Arbogast, the Deputy from the Lower Rhine, who was Rector of the University of Strasbourg, after describing the situation in the educational establishments, where mediocre textbooks were used that were more than a century behind the times, and after pointing out that "the lack or scarcity of elementary textbooks has been up to the present one of the greatest obstacles blocking the improvement of instruction," proposed "that the representatives of the people ask learned men to write books and to dream of the glory of being the creators of the present generation and of preparing the happiness of future generations."[132]

The proposed decree on the general organization of public instruction presented by Condorcet to the National Assembly in 1792 stated, "The immediate composition of elementary books that will be used for instruction in primary schools will be ordered. These books will be written according to the best method of instruction that current advances in the sciences suggest and according to the principles of liberty, of equality, and of the purity of customs, and of abnegation in public affairs, all of which are consecrated in the constitution." Farther on this same decree orders, "Books of readings will be composed for citizens on farms and in the cities, which are to be limited to the first grade of instruction. These works, which will differ according to the age and sex of those for whom they are intended, will remind each person of his rights and his responsibilities, as well as provide the knowledge he needs according to the place he occupies in society."[133]

Most likely these precedents influenced Bolívar in the writing of the passages on the Commission on Education. In fact, Articles 3, 4, 5, and 6, continuing what had been stated in Article 2 on the publication of educational manuals for mothers, decree as follows: "In addition to these instructions, the Commission will sponsor the publication in our language of foreign works most appropriate to enlighten the nation in these matters, deriving wisdom from them and the observations and adjustments that come with them" (Article 3). "It will encourage learned men and all those who write and publish original works about them in accordance with our usages, customs, and government" (Article 4). "Since the Commission itself, better than anybody else, will collect within a short time all the facts and knowledge necessary for such a work, it will compose and publish one that will serve at the same time as a stimulus to other persons to occupy themselves with this task and as a source of learning for everybody" (Article 5). "It will not stint on the means or spare the expense or withhold sacrifices that it can use in adapting its knowledge to the end of its being acquired; it will commission, then, zealous, informed, and broad-minded men who are traveling, investigating the entire world, and gathering all kinds of intelligence on the subject" (Article 6).

The fact that five of the thirteen articles on the attributions of the Commission on Education are devoted to this subject

would seem to indicate the importance given by the Liberator
to educational books even though they made Rousseau furious.
The value of this idea of Bolívar's is found in the possibility it
affords of compensating for the lack of teachers with the learned
inspirations contained in the manuals, which are thus durable
teachers to which it is possible to turn at any time in order to
consult them. Of course it could be argued that in order to read
the manuals it was necessary to have a teacher charged with
teaching how to read—falling into a vicious circle.

Primers outlining elementary principles might even be useful
in helping parents in the understanding and guidance of their
children, so that the home might recover its functions, which had
been so battered by the development of a civilization that has
made of the factory the place of concentration and of contact,
while the children are abandoned. The thought of Bolívar on this
subject continues to be, not only relevant, but demanding of immediate application, with whatever adjustments may be advisable
on account of the changes brought by time.[134]

7. ORIENTATION OF THE CURRICULUM

The plan of education suggested in Article 7 of the section on
the Commission on Education does not contain any novel ideas,
since it refers to elementary subjects that had been considered
by the educational experts of the time as essential to the training of the citizen: "reading, writing, arithmetic, and grammar,
instruction in the rights of man and of the citizen," this last being
a subject that France raised to the level of a compulsory ritual
for all Frenchmen. However, Bolívar's proposal added that the
student must absorb "the ideas and sentiments of honor and probity," something insisted on repeatedly in the moral education
of Venezuelans, as well as "love of country, of laws, and of work;
respect for all men, for old people, for officials; and devotion to
the government."[135]

In his speech before the Congress of Angostura, which served
as an explanation of the motives behind the proposed Constitution submitted to that illustrious Assembly, Bolívar had said,

"Love of country, love of the laws, love for officials, are the noble passions which the soul of a republican must exclusively absorb. Venezuelans love their country, yes, but they do not love its laws; because these have been noxious and were the source of evil. They have also not been able to love the officials, because they were iniquitous, and the new ones are hardly known in the career in which they have entered. If there is not hallowed respect for the country, for the laws, and for the officials, the society is a confusion, a state of single combat of man against man, of body against body."[136]

The curriculum he suggested thus tended to expose the minds of students to the elementary instruction required for promoting moral principles and respect for laws and officials, since these principles and this respect are identical with the stability of democratic institutions.

These Bolivarian formulations are the inspiration for what is now known in the curriculum under the name of "civics" or "social studies," which, as we have seen before, have their antecedents in the ideas of Rousseau, Diderot, and especially in those expounded by Talleyrand, Condorcet, Lakanal, and others who were concerned in a noteworthy way with this theme when presenting plans for educational reform during the French Revolution.

8. THE BUILDING OF SCHOOLS

Articles 8 and 9 placed among the obligations of the commission the elaboration of a plan for building schools, in which the structural requirements of these establishments and the locations they should be given would be indicated. In Article 8 it was said that "the form, proportion, and location of those establishments will be whatever is most suited to their purpose, and not only will solidity and size be considered in them but also elegance, cleanliness, comfort, and the recreation of young people." Article 9, with a kind of attention to minute detail that is very current, points out that the plan for building schools ought to take into account, in addition to the number of schools necessary, the provinces where they should be constructed and the location each one should occupy within the provinces, "calculating for this purpose all the advantages of place, how easy it will be to bring all the children together there, the healthiness of the terrain, the abundance and quality of food."[137]

Specifications of the material conditions of the school had been forgotten or postponed, but the school, according to Comenius, should be located "by preference in a pleasant place, adorned with the shadow of fruit trees and shade trees, lawns and images; a place so spacious that the entire number of children will fit into it, with each class by itself."[138] Even before then Juan Luis Vives had foreseen that "the establishing of the school is the first thing that needs attention. The first thing that has to be assured is the healthfulness of the place, which should be such that the students do not have to desert it suddenly on account of the fear of epidemics . . . It has to be seen then that an abundance of healthful foods is easily available . . . Further, the place should be apart from all concentrations of people, especially of workmen who in their respective labors make a great racket, among whom are carpenters, ironmongers, bricklayers . . ." But he warned, "In order to avoid this disadvantage, I would not choose a place so rich in verdure and so pleasant that it would lure the students to frequent absences from their studies."[139]

As we read the mentioned Articles 8 and 9, we find them to be valid for the present situation. The ideas that Bolívar many times put into writing are pushed aside by contemporary architects and urban developers because they are concerned more with money-making ends than with the interests of education, when they are not simply being driven by the dangerous conditions that result from the unplanned growth of cities or from the little importance that is given in them to the location of schools.

9. VITAL STATISTICS

Another idea truly novel at the time and even today not applied in all its fullness is that contained in Article 12, according to which "each year the Commission will publish tables or exact and detailed statements on the births and deaths of children, on their physical constitution, on their health and illnesses, on their progress, inclinations, qualities, and individual talents, so that all these observations shall be made to serve the teachers, priests, doctors, provincial agents, noted citizens, and the authorities, all of whom, beginning with the President himself, shall be guided by them in the matter of education."[140]

These vital and cultural statistics, so necessary in order to draw up a balance sheet of the advances made in a country, have come to be completely available only in some of the more advanced nations, but in all nations they are indispensable for the planning of development in education and the devotion of attention to the health of the population, especially when it comes to anticipating future advances and the needs that will have to be confronted. Statistical information "on their progress, inclinations, qualities, and individual talents" was meant to be used for the purpose of making manifest the need to utilize the natural tendencies of the best individuals for the benefit of the public, an idea which is the basis of vocational and professional education, which only now is coming to be accepted among us, although very slowly and in an uncertain way.

The importance that Bolívar gave to statistics is made emphatic in the recommendation made to the teachers of his nephew, to whom he said, "Statistics is a necessary course of study in the times through which we are passing, and it is my wish that my nephew learn this subject." More than a hundred years were to pass before statistics came to be included in the curriculum of our universities, although basic notions of the technique were given in commercial schools.

10. WHAT IS LIVING AND WHAT IS DEAD IN THE COMMISSION ON EDUCATION

The Bolivarian idea of the Commission on Education, or of the principles of government-sponsored education introduced into the Constitution, was supported by German teachers in 1848, that is, twenty-nine years later, but was accepted only at the time of the so-called doctrine of "the rationalization of the law" in the European constitutions that followed the First World War, of which the prime example is the German Weimar Constitution, and in the Mexican Constitution of 1917. In Venezuela it was made into law for the first time in the Constitution of 1947, where the resolution passed by the Venezuelan Federation of Teachers at its eleventh national convention, which met in 1946 on the island of Margarita, was adopted. The Constitution of 1961 reproduces these principles.

A section devoted to education appears in almost all the constitutions of Latin America, but it is forgotten that this constitutional provision has its roots in the fundamental charter of Bolívar of 1819, which contained the Commission on Education among its proposals. Nevertheless, the enunciation of educational principles in modern constitutions is not the same thing as the organization of a council similar to the commission to direct education proposed by Bolívar. Such an idea was valid at a time when ministries of education did not exist. In our own day, however, it seems out of place in the Cuban Constitution of 1940 and the Costa Rican Constitution of 1948. The National Council of Education in Argentina and the various Councils on Instruction that operate in Uruguay, although they are not constitutionally founded but were created by the respective laws on the subject passed in both these countries at the end of the last century, also seem to conspire against the unity of the general orientation in education. In Uruguay there are four autonomous councils separately directing each of the branches of instruction: primary and normal schools, secondary schools, technical schools, and universities. The appearance of ministries of education coincides with the growth of greater governmental interest in and attention to popular education. This explains why, even in England, where such activities are assigned to municipal administrations, the transference of educational management to national organizations, under the control of recently created ministries of education, seems to be in progress.

Part Three

BOLÍVAR ON THE SUBJECTS AND METHODS OF INSTRUCTION

1. THE ABILITY OF THE STUDENT

Other writings by Bolívar, which are not related to educational politics but which are concerned with procedures of instruction and the internal organization of the school, are of secondary importance, although they do contain solutions to educational problems and principles worthy of being taken into account.

In the instructions in which he condensed the method he thought should be followed in the education of his nephew Fernando Bolívar, to which reference has already been made and which will be analyzed later on, the principle of the adaptation of instruction to the conditions of development and the abilities of the student is confirmed. He takes up this same theme in Article 12 of the Commission on Education. In speaking of vital statistics, he asks that in the tables to be drawn up the record should contain, along with information on other conditions of the child, data on "his progress, inclinations, qualities, and individual talents."

This is an ancient principle formulated by Quintilian, who is quoted by Bolívar. In his *Institutio oratoria* the Hispanic-Latin author said, "because in the way that bottles with a narrow mouth do not receive any of the liquor that is thrown in their direction but are filled when it is dropped in little by little or drop by drop, so in this same way one has to take into account what the talent of the child is able to receive. Because if they are things that exceed his capacity, he will not learn anything, in as much as it does not take in so much."[141]

In the sixteenth century the noted Spanish educator Juan Luis Vives recommended, "Let the teachers come together in secret four times a year for the purpose of exchanging impressions about the possibilities of their respective students and to discuss the art they ought to apply to each one according to the competence each demonstrates."[142] And a little later, in the seventeenth century, Comenius was quite explicit on this delicate subject. In *Didactica magna,* the greatest book on education of its time, and to which Rousseau owed so much, Comenius said, "In the same way that the nature of herbs, trees, and animals differs, and that some must be treated in one way and others in different ways so that they will not all let themselves be applied equally to the same ends, so human minds too are like that. There is no lack of eager minds that understand and decipher everything; but neither do we fail to find others that easily become dull and are inaccessible to certain subjects . . . There is no reason to incite the progress of the students against the will of Minerva . . . If none of the students is educated and instructed contrary to his inclination, there will be no occasion for contrariness and displeasure, which redound with greater force upon the mind; with greater facility each one advances in that to which he is inclined by his natural instinct . . ."[143]

Diderot, after referring to the sequence of studies and to the accommodation of instruction to its utility, points out that one must "adjust instruction to age and lessons to the average capacity of the mind." Later on, in a different place, he says, "All students do not possess an equal aptitude for everything. One, endowed with a prodigious memory, will make great progress in history and geography. Others, more meditative, will easily combine numbers and spaces and will distinguish themselves, almost without work, in arithmetic and geometry. If instruction has only one unique objective, the student whom nature has endowed with little or no aptitude for that course of study will be constantly humiliated and discouraged."[144]

Rousseau develops the theme of vocation and capacity in *Emile*. He speaks of the possibility of achieving advantages with education when the child possesses a special ingenuity for an art and if a previous study of "his hobby, inclinations, and likes" is applied to him. And he warned against the general error of confusing the imitative spirit common to man and the monkey, and which mechanically incite them to do whatever they see done without knowing what its purpose is, with an irrepressible inclination to some art or other. Rousseau also referred to what is a problem of contemporary life, that of those persons who, forced by necessity, practice an art or profession for which they have no "special talent" simply because they have applied themselves to it from their earliest years. However, the Genevan is in agreement with the idea, which is today a commonplace, that while "perseverance up to a certain point takes the place of ability," it cannot be a substitute for genuine talent. For Rousseau there is a great difference between being strongly attracted to an occupation and being naturally good at it, and this latter is the condition that the educator has to take into account in the orientation and guidance of his students, taking into consideration the intimate structure of their capacities and their sense of calling.[145] That is the problem posed by Bolívar in the education of his nephew Fernando and in other parts of his educational thought that have already been mentioned. That was also the concern of the men of the Enlightenment. Goethe, who in many aspects of his thought took his inspiration from Rousseau, said in *The Apprenticeship of Wilhelm Meister*, "Education must be founded on natural tendencies. In man the first and last thing is doing, and nothing can be done without having a disposition for it, without instinct impelling us to do it."

Educators of the present day consider the problems derived from the capacities and the sense of vocation to be fundamental elements for orienting the educational process. Today it is believed that whoever chooses badly in the choice of a profession suffers consequences that can be fatal when the occupation does not suit his personality. This affects the psychic balance of the individual and leads him into constant boredom and annoyance that degenerates into nervous fatigue, a feeling of frustration that can be avoided through a felicitous professional orientation.

2. THE TEACHING OF LANGUAGES

Space is given to the principle that study of one's native language ought to precede the learning of foreign languages. This theme was constantly the cause of heated discussions, above all when the learning of Latin was compulsory and the national language was disregarded. Somebody said that whoever is ignorant of his own language can hardly know a foreign language. For Bolívar the study of living languages should take precedence over the knowledge of dead languages. It is true also that ancient languages did not figure in the curriculum given in *Emile;* but even so it seems to me that Bolívar, when organizing the curriculum of his nephew, could have found his inspiration in Diderot and in La Chalotais more than in Rousseau.

In fact, Diderot complained that his contemporaries looked upon French literature with disdain, and he proposed that the study of French be given preference, along with two foreign languages, "English for science and German for warfare." Diderot argued, "It is a significant matter to know whether the exclusive study of dead languages is worth the time that is devoted to them or whether this precious time of childhood might not be employed in more important occupations . . ." Later on he added, "I believe that the study of dead languages could be considerably shortened and mixed somewhat with useful knowledge. In general, too much space and importance has been given in the schools to the study of words. I believe that the schools ought to give some notion of all the knowledge necessary to a citizen, from legislation to mechanical arts, which have contributed so much to the progress and adornment of society, and in these arts I include the professions of the most obscure class of citizens. The pageant of human industry is in itself great and satisfactory; it is good to know the different contributions that each person makes to the progress of society."[146]

La Chalotais also included "music and dance, which ought to form part of the education of persons placed above the common." The Liberator, in spite of his maintaining that it was not necessary for his nephew to learn music unless it turned out that he had a passion for this art, recommended, on the other hand, the practice of dance, "which is the poetry of movement and which gives grace and ease to people, at the same time that it is a hygienic exercise in a temperate climate."[147]

3. THE RETROSPECTIVE METHOD IN THE TEACHING OF HISTORY

Just as Diderot did, so La Chalotais too maintained that the teaching of history ought to begin with contemporary events. Diderot said, "I believe that the study of history could begin with the study of the history of our own nation, but that this, as well as the study of other nations, ought to begin with times most close at hand, going backwards later to the centuries of fable or mythology." This is the sentiment of Grotius. "In general," he said, "do not begin with remote events that are immaterial to us, but with the most important things that deeply concern us, and advance later little by little to the origins of time."[148]

La Chalotais, on his side, reasoned, "I would wish that histories of all the nations be composed for each one of the children, that these histories cover all centuries and above all these latest centuries, that these latest be more detailed, that the histories of these centuries be read before the history of remote centuries."[149]

Bolívar said that "history, like languages, ought to be studied beginning with what is contemporary, in order to go backward by degrees until arriving at the obscure times of the fable."[150]

On the contrary, for Rousseau this idea of the contemporaneity of the history that is studied in the schools lacked all significance. He said that adolescence is an appropriate time to learn history, in which the student "will read into hearts without the lesson of philosophy: being thus a mere spectator, he will look into hearts without interest or passion, as a judge, neither as an accomplice nor as an accuser." His idea was "to teach [Emile] to observe men at a distance, in other times and other countries, in such a way that he might look upon the scene without being able ever to act in it."[151]

This idea of Rousseau's is contradictory to that expressed by Bolívar, who proposed beginning with the present, perhaps with living men and recent events, setting up a mirror to the emotions in order to inspire heroic deeds in his nephew and to encourage him, who was the student to whom his instructions referred, to continue along the path traced by Bolívar himself and by the liberators of America, who even then were unfolding their actions upon the wide stage of a continent for the conquest of freedom. No other example could be of greater educative value, nor was there any need to seek in the characters of Plutarch or in the histories of the Greeks and Romans or of any of the peoples of Europe for a more lively and fascinating lesson for a young man. Neither the action of Leonidas at Thermopylae, nor Caesar's conquest of Gaul, nor Hannibal's passage through the Alps, is in any way worthy of comparison with the amazing exploit of

Bolívar's campaign across the Andes, which Marius André describes as "one of the most extraordinary in the history of all the nations."

In order to shape the mind of his student, Rousseau pronounced against recent history. Indeed, he said, "I leave aside contemporary history, not only because it does not have a marked physiognomy and our men are all alike, but because our historians, concerned only with showing themselves off to advantage, are not thinking of anything but of making portraits with extremely vivid colors that have no resemblance to anything in reality. In general, the ancients painted fewer portraits and expended less wit and put more sense into their judgments; and yet extraordinary discernment is necessary in order to choose among them."[152]

Bolívar's bold appeal to examples from recent history, as well as his suggestion for employing a more rational method, one in touch with the interests and the emotions of the student, was a way of bringing the student as a participant into the work that was being realized in the world around him and in contributing to which he who learns would recognize himself, not as a spectator or as a judge, as Rousseau asked, but as a coresponsible person. In that sense history is being converted into a task for everybody because everybody makes it and lives it, and when they learn it they unite the action of the present with whatever actions in other times were making history too, and with their making they inherit the patrimony that the nation and the world preserve as an inheritance, which grows or declines depending upon the actions of the heirs.

The methodology of the retrogressive way of teaching history has been opposed, but in modern pedagogy it is accepted under the name of retrospective or regressive method, urging upon its partisans the necessity of uniting the teaching of history with that of geography, in the study of which the student begins with what is immediately around him in space, in order to pass from the school to the city, to the province, to the nation, to the continent, to the world. Manuel B. Cossío, without passing judgment on the method, explained the way in which history was taught in the Free Teaching Association of Madrid.

"A beginning is made," Cossío said, "principally by making note of those most remarkable contrasts that different degrees of culture of different people offer among themselves, especially the two extremes of the series: observing the most characteristic features of *our own state of culture* in all human ends (science, art, religion, politics, etc.) parallel with those that these same ends offer in savage peoples.

"A study of contrasts of this kind (in which a great deal of time is spent) constitutes, at bottom, a general picture in major outline of contemporary civilization, as well as that of the origins of civilization. In this way, an attempt is made to initiate a certain effort at system, embracing from the very first and all at once as a unity, in the way that the law of knowing suggests, the whole historical process included between its two extremes: the savage condition and present-day culture, since this is the most vivid, real, and perceptible contrast that the child, in an immediate way, is able to observe. History for him begins by being the efforts that men have made to pass from one to the other of those two states."[153]

The present discussion validates the ideas of this retrospective method. It is sometimes forgotten that a method has value only in relation to the teacher who uses it and, as Rousseau said, to the interest that the teacher awakens in the student and to his "desire to learn."

Bolívar thought that "geography and cosmography ought to be the first knowledge that a child acquires,"[154] perhaps on account of the ties they have with history, since this unfolds within the terrain that is offered it by the world. For La Chalotais, for the same reason, the teaching of geography is not separate from the teaching of history; it is from this fact that his suggestion of commencing with contemporary history arises.

4. THE TEACHING OF MATHEMATICS

Perhaps there are also influences from Diderot and La Chalotais in other aspects of the curriculum recommended by Bolívar for his nephew Fernando. Indeed, as is known, Diderot gave priority to the teaching of the sciences. According to Diderot, "It is easier to learn arithmetic and elementary geometry than to learn to read." Even before then he had said, "No objects exist as general as number and space. To know geometry and to be a geometrician are two different things. To only a few men is it given to be a geometrician, but to all is it given to learn arithmetic and geometry. For that nothing more is needed than a bit of common sense, and the child of thirteen who is not capable of this study is no good for anything and ought to be thrown out of school."[155]

On his part La Chalotais placed the study of geometry and mathematics in the curriculum of the primary school, for he believed that geometry did not offer anything that was not available to the senses and palpable. In the curriculum of La Chalotais, which would now be considered a curriculum for secondary schools, we find: (1) literature, Latin, and the humanities; (2) continuation of history, of geometry, of mathematics, and of natural history; (3) literary and esthetic criticism, logic, and metaphysics; (4) techniques of invention; (5) ethics.

Bolívar too offers the suggestion that "it is never too early for the knowledge of the exact sciences, because they teach us how to analyze everything, passing from the known to the unknown, and in that way we learn to think and to reason logically."[156] Perhaps remembering his own study of mathematics at the San Fernando Academy in Madrid, Bolívar insists again on the need to consider the suitability of studies to the talents of the student. "The capacity of the student," he observes, "for the study of calculus ought to be kept in mind, for not everybody is particularly good at mathematics." And he concludes, "Generally everybody can learn geometry and understand it; but the same thing does not happen with algebra and integral and differential calculus."[157]

As may be deduced from these quotations, there is a great similarity between the ideas of Bolívar and those expressed by Diderot. Diderot still believed that "geometry is the best and the simplest of all logics, the most appropriate for developing flexibility in judgment and reasoning."[158] But we find this same idea, which is at present known by the name of "transfer of learning" or "formal training," whose principles are in open bankruptcy, in *The Republic*, of Plato, where we read that "as experience shows, whoever has studied geometry is infinitely quicker at picking up other things than somebody who has not studied it."[159] Quintilian devotes Chapter IX of his *Institutio oratoria* to geometry. There, among other things, he asserts that geometry serves the orator for deducing a consequence from given premises and for discovering by way of demonstration the falsity of an apparent truth. And he concludes, "Thus, since the orator has to speak on all subjects, he cannot go for long without geometry."[160]

John Locke, priding himself on the practical and utilitarian spirit of the English, explains that "of all the sciences of abstract reasoning, arithmetic is the easiest and should, therefore, be the first to which one ought to be accustomed, and it is of such general usage in the whole of life and business that one can hardly do anything without it."[161] He also said that some parts of geometry are necessary for the man engaged in commerce. In his judgment, "for helping the student to reason and to think well, there is nothing like the serious study of the mathematical sciences."[162]

Bolívar's thought, in so far as it is concerned with the curriculum, has valuable antecedents, which do not appear at all in the work of Rousseau, not because Rousseau would have nothing to do with the study of mathematics, but because his course of study is carried on in contact with things and as a means of developing the senses and outside of all systematic plan. "I have said," Rousseau asserted, "that geometry is not within reach of children, but the fault is ours. We are not aware that our method is not theirs and that what for us is the art of discussing is for them the art of seeing. Instead of giving them our method, it would be better for us to try to take on theirs, because our way of learning geometry is as much a matter of imagination as of reasoning."[163]

5. APPRENTICESHIP IN A PROFESSION OR VOCATION

Insisting on the education of his nephew Fernando and considering the requirements of his nephew's possible vocation, Bo-

lívar said, "Since it is very hard to determine where practice
ends and theory begins, if his inclination leads him to decide to
learn some craft or trade I would applaud him, since there is an
abundance of doctors and lawyers among us, but we are lacking
in good mechanics and farmers, who are what the country needs
in order to advance in prosperity and well-being."[164]

This preference for a manual occupation in the education of a
child of a distinguished family, as that of the Liberator was,
implied a sharp break with existing customs, a liberating position,
since colonial practices had brought about a supreme contempt
for the so-called base professions to give preference to what were
named the noble arts: soldiering, the priesthood, and the liberal
careers (law, engineering, and so on).

It is true that the lawyer Miguel José Sanz and Simón Rodríguez, the latter Bolívar's teacher, had come out against this practice, but both of them, along with Pestalozzi, were referring to
the education of the common people, of the poor who live from
their work. Rousseau too wanted Emile to learn a manual trade,
in which the mastery exercised by the hands would be predominant, for the purpose of developing skills. "I am not asking for
a profession," said Rousseau, "but a genuine trade, a merely
mechanical art, in which the hands work more than the head,
through which nobody would grow rich, but which would place
whoever knows it in the condition of not needing to grow rich."[165]
But Rousseau was thinking fundamentally that Emile ought to
be prepared in the event that, owing to the revolutions, he were
to lose his wealth and the means of subsistence proper to a well-
off person. This trade would be for Emile a kind of security
against the revolution, in case it were to leave him without riches.
If such an event were not to occur, he would never have the
opportunity to practice his trade. Nevertheless, Rousseau did
maintain that "work is an obligation of social man," and that
"rich or poor, strong or weak, every idle citizen is a thief." Even
though he believed that there is no honor without usefulness,
he always asked that one take "an honorable occupation," as if
all of them were not honorable by reason of their social utility.
Emile, placed in the situation of having to choose a trade, ought
to take its cleanliness into account, and Rousseau picks out, as
clean and worthy of preference, cabinetmaking, the manufacture

of mathematical instruments, lenses, telescopes, and so forth.[166]

Locke, who was many times quoted by Bolívar, when concerning himself with the education of the English gentleman, writing before Rousseau, also came out in favor of the learning of a trade. "I would wish," said Locke, "that my gentleman learn a trade—yes, a manual trade: even that he learn two or three if he wishes, but especially one." But that trade was not intended to serve the gentleman as a means of gaining his livelihood or as a way of influencing the life of the community, but as a diversion, as an opportunity for rest and exercise, like what is now known by the name of "hobby," useful or necessary for the health, "because the manual arts, which in order to be learned and in order to be practiced require the labor of the body, have as their effect, not only increasing our skill and ability through practice, but also strengthening our health, above all those in which the work is done in the open air."[167]

Bolívar's ideas about apprenticeship in a vocation are totally different from the position of Locke and Rousseau, because it starts out from the analysis of a social reality. When he asks that preference be given to a manual art, it is because he considers this most useful and necessary for the solution of the problems of his people. He does not treat the occupation as a personal acquisition that may have some eventual benefit or solve some problem for the individual, not even as an educative technique for acquiring skill, nor in order to conquer the presuppositions that make that vocation contemptible, as Rousseau wished, nor as a pleasing entertainment or recreation, as Locke preferred, but as an activity of collective service, because "we are lacking in good mechanics and farmers, who are what the country needs in order to advance in prosperity and well-being."

This way of looking at the choice of an occupation, in addition to its modernity, indicates how Bolívar, over and above personal satisfaction and the opportunity for improvement, sought that each American, beginning with the persons he most cared for, devote himself with his labors and his talents to the creation of the economic and social conditions within which, along with political freedom, men would be able to enjoy security. This idea is urgently relevant at the present time, when an accelerated process of economic development is being carried out on our continent, which can be realized only by men educated for achieving this objective, who are not the products of an intellectualistic school without attachment to the real needs of the nation.

6. ON TRAINING THE MEMORY

With keen insight into methods of learning, not yet very well developed in his time due to the scarcity of scientific knowledge about the processes of the mind, Bolívar pointed out that "the memory, as well as skill in calculation, is subject to strengthening through practice." According to Bolívar, "The memory ought to be exercised as much as possible, but without ever tiring it."[168] These notions are in agreement with the statements of Quintilian, for whom the memory "increases with exercise just as all other things do . . . but it gets weary when it is overburdened."[169] They are, however, in clear contradiction to Rousseau, for whom "Emile will never learn anything by memory, not even fables, even though they be those of La Fontaine, with all their merits; because the words of fables are themselves fables, just as the words of history are history."[170]

"Although the memory and the power of reasoning," Rousseau maintained, "are two faculties essentially distinct, in spite of that neither of them can be truly developed without the other. Before the age of reason, the child does not receive ideas but images. He is not, for that reason, capable of formulating judgments that are obtained by the comparison of conceived ideas." Therefore, he concludes by saying, "that, since children are not capable of judgment, they have no true memory."[171]

The Swiss philosopher was reacting against the rote learning that was the dominant method of education in his time, a method in which words were taught by means of words themselves, requiring the child to acquire items of knowledge that were incomprehensible to him. Thus Rousseau said, "If nature endows the child with a kind of flexibility that makes him apt to receive all kinds of impressions, this is not in order that the names of kings, dates, terms of heraldry, of courtly life, of geometry, should be imprinted in him, along with all those words that mean nothing at his age, that are not useful at any other, and which overwhelm his childhood, making it sterile and unhappy." His idea of learning was functional, having no relation to books, but tied to nature and to the immediate interests of the child. "The kind of memory that a child might have," he asserted, "will not long be idle because it does not learn from books. It retains and recalls everything it sees and everything it hears and everything that comes to him is the book with which, without thinking about it, he is continually enriching his memory up to the point where his reason is able to utilize it."[172]

But, however fine Rousseau's exaggerations might have been as a reaction against formalism in instruction, Bolívar was not able to follow them, since his experience had revealed to him the advantages of a memory enrichened through the constant and systematic labor of learning. He takes advantage of his own great store of ideas, of which Perú de Lacroix has spoken to us, in those "quotations . . . always chosen and appropriate to the purpose" in which he showed himself proud of his extensive reading.[173] It was his affirmation that "the memory that is too quick is a brilliant faculty, but it redounds to the detriment of understanding." From motives such as this, he formulated his recommendation: "The child who demonstrates too great a facility for retaining by memorization ought to be taught those things that oblige him to meditate, such as solving problems and working out equations; vice versa, those who are slow in retention ought to be taught to learn things by memory and to recite compositions chosen from the great poets."[174]

The French psychologist Alfred Binet, to whom so many important studies on memory are due, made it clear at the beginning of this century that "the memory is at its height during childhood, and it is necessary, above all, to cultivate it at this age and to take advantage of its plasticity in order to impress upon it the important memories, the decisive memories that will be found necessary later on in life."[175]

The idea of the progressive enrichment of the memory is discussed by some modern psychologists, but the impossibility of learning without a memory to supply the materials to be learned remains an open question. In order to train the memory, one tries to develop it by reinforcing its natural conditions, with the objective of making it more capable as an instrument for the acquisition of knowledge and as a basis for the integration of new ideas and new experiences, which are added to those already acquired.

Bolívar's methodological idea about the different pace that has to be adopted for those who are quick and for those who are slow in memorizing should be understood as a way of exposure to the material through reflection and analysis for the former and through practice in acceleration for the latter. Perhaps what he proposed was avoiding in those who are quick what is now known by the name of accumulation, a phenomenon produced when one tries to learn a great quantity of material in a short time, in that way blocking understanding, because the processes of learning are mechanized and the reasoning processes are weakened. Without doubt Bolívar was intuitively referring to this kind of memorization, since it is this that "redounds to the detriment of understanding," as we have already seen.

However, it is necessary to observe—not of course for those who are experts in the field—that the rate of learning depends upon differences in character and, as William Stern notes, the slow learner can be more complete and more critical than the fast learner. "While the fast learner can surpass the other in the power of retention over a brief span of time, the labor of the slow learner usually is of greater scope in the long run."[176]

The balanced way of utilizing the memory proposed by Bolívar, with the corrections that may be suggested by the new psychological science, is applicable today and, even when it involves a reaction against the abuse of the memory, recognizes the inestimable value of that instrument, which ought not be utilized in an irrational and immoderate way.

7. THE TEACHING OF READING

In methodological matters, Bolívar gave his opinion about the best way of teaching how to read and indicated a method that begins with exercises in the awareness of the letters, then in the pronunciation of syllables, but without spelling, passing later to reading from a book.[177]

The teaching of reading has presented and always presents grave problems, which the methodologists try to solve by an adequate use of different resources. Already Quintilian, to whom I have referred several times because Bolívar studied him with the thoroughness that the Hispanic-Latin teacher deserves, criticized the way of teaching reading of his times, which was by learning the names and the order of the letters, and came out in favor of a kind of game with the shape of each letter in marble "or some other material of which the age may be fonder, and which they will find pleasure in handling, watching, and pointing out by name."[178] John Locke believed that play ought to serve as the basis of the education of children and, like Quintilian, proposed that various toys be given to them by means of which they would, with pleasure and little by little, learn the alphabet and, later on, writing.

Rousseau made fun of these methodological judgments, appealing to the supreme motive force behind all learning, which is present interest. Commenting on Locke, Rousseau says, "He holds it to be very important to discover the best methods for teaching how to read; picture books and maps are created, and the child's room is turned into a printing shop. Locke wants the child to learn how to read with dice. Isn't that an exquisite invention? What a pity! There is a way more certain than all of them, one that is always forgotten: the desire to learn. Instill this desire in the child; then you may leave aside the cardboard and the dice, for every method will be good for him."[179]

The methodologists have gone on inventing systems for teaching how to read, without excluding games, dice, and the picture books used by Comenius. Synthetic methods[180] (like that proposed by Bolívar, because it goes from the literal elements to syllables, to words, to sentences), analytic methods, eclectic methods. Comenius proposed that reading and writing be taught simultaneously, just as they have come into practice, but at the present time some teachers are in favor of learning to read first, in order to simplify the process of learning, relieving it of one complication.

These investigations prove the lack of rationality in some points of view, but many people go on learning how to read by psy-

chologically inappropriate methods, which are, however, effica-
cious according to the abilities of those who apply them—all of
which indicates, in effect, that what is important is not the system
followed but the aim pursued in teaching and the results obtained, which undoubtedly, can be more bountiful with the
utilization of a scientific method, but even the value of such a
method may be invalidated in the hands of an unskilled teacher.

Bolívar's opinion about the procedures for teaching reading to
children, although he was not a methodologist, is only one indication of his eagerness to make instruction part and parcel
of the work of wise government and of the rational use of
liberty within the legal organizations established by the republic.

8. KNOWLEDGE OF UNIVERSAL LEGISLATION

The expressions of the Liberator on the teaching of Roman law,
as a basis for the knowledge of universal legislation, are related
to the curriculum suggested by Diderot and to the ideas of La
Chalotais. This concern, as we have seen, was fundamental in
the men of the Encyclopedia and was carried into the juridical
formulations of the French Revolution, which put forward the
training of the citizen as the essential purpose of education. In
fact, all the curriculums suggested in the proposals presented to
the Assembly, especially those of Talleyrand and Condorcet, advanced the notion that the training of the citizen should be accomplished by means of learning elementary ideas of law and
especially the principles of the Constitution and the Table of the
Rights of Man—without, however, making any reference to Roman law.[181] Diderot, in his essay on the state of studies in Russia,
said, "It would be desirable if a catechism were taken equally
from ethics and from politics, that is, little books in which elementary notions about the laws of the country and the duties
of the citizens were explained for the instruction and use of the
people." Already in commenting on Article 7 of the Commission
on Education, I have pointed out that Bolívar too places among

the subjects of the curriculum instruction on "the rights and duties of the man and citizen and the ideas and sentiments of
honor and probity, love of country, of the laws, and of work,
respect for parents, for the aged, for the officials, and adherence
to the government."[182]

9. SOCIAL CONTACT AS A MEANS
OF EDUCATION

In opposition to the opinions held by Rousseau—for whom the
education of Emile was to be realized outside of contact with
society, since society perverts everything; for whom, as we have
seen, man is born good and pure and it is society that places
notions of perversity within him—in opposition to these opinions,
Bolívar recommended, in the final paragraph on the method
suggested for the education of his nephew Fernando, "inspiring
him with the liking of cultivated society, where the fair sex exercises its beneficent influence; and that respect for men of years,
knowledge, and social position, which makes an enchantment of
youth, associating it with the hopes of the future." This Bolivarian
idea of education by means of social contact, or, rather, by means
of living together, is of great modernity, since today it is believed
that it is society which educates, that the teacher is only an agent
of the community, and that the school is a conditioned place
where the student acquires in a systematic way the knowledge
that society itself considers necessary and indispensable. The
liking for cultivated society, of which Bolívar speaks, and the
beneficent influence that woman exercises in it, is already a way
of orienting the education of the young man toward life itself,
without taking from him the value of his own experience, and
a way of confronting the dangers that this orientation prepares
him for, dangers that were described in the observations of
Rousseau. But Bolívar's suggestions are opposed to Rousseau's
proposal that Emile be educated in isolation from the social environment, and above all from living together with woman, who
might disorient him, when, in reality, it is in contact with the fair

sex that mutual respect and the ideas of refinement due to this respect are learned.

La Chalotais had observed, among the deficiencies of education, that it had no relation to sound customs, so that, after the student has suffered the fatigue and tedium of the schools, "he finds himself with the necessity of learning what the common duties of all men are."[183] It is this deficiency that Bolívar's suggestions are intended to correct.

10. THE SCHOOL AND THE TEACHER UNDER NEW NAMES

Some of Bolívar's educational ideas in his writings on public education included in the *Obras completas,* to which reference has already been made, ought to be emphasized since they indicate a noteworthy concern for the diffusion of education, making it general to all the population. Those ideas are related to the activity he carried on throughout the continent in an effort to popularize culture—thereby remaining faithful to the principles propagated by the men of the Enlightenment and of the French Revolution, especially by Condorcet, Talleyrand, Mirabeau, and others.

It is to be supposed that at that time the existing schools were scarce and of very inferior quality, and that in them colonial practices had converted the teacher into a kind of little tyrant who, with methods of compulsion, tried to validate the expression, "Learning goes in with blood." Out of this circumstance the Liberator became interested, not only in eradicating those procedures, but in changing even the name of the establishment where teaching was administered and of the person charged with teaching, in spite of the fact that it could be alleged, as he himself pointed out, that changing names means nothing if what the original words designated continues to exist. He proposed that the school be called *society* and that the teacher be called *director*. But these names are of little importance. What is more important are the functions that Bolívar assigns to the director or teacher, and the qualities that he requires of this leader of childhood, who in opposition to the previous type comes close to the present-day notion of the teacher, according to the definitions given by modern educators such as Kerschesteiner, who defined education as a profession of love. "The educational Eros is he who leads most rapidly to a most profound educational understanding."[184] For Bolívar, the "director of a school [the teacher] is a generous man and a lover of his country who, sacrificing his repose and his liberty, devotes himself to the generous exercise of creating citizens for the state, who will defend it, make it famous, sanctify it, beautify it, and who will engender others as worthy as himself." These qualities of the teacher make him worthy of the title "The Well-Deserving of the Fatherland" and on that account "merits the veneration and the appreciation of the government." Rousseau expressed the opinion, speaking of Poland, that "its teachers ought to be only Poles, all married, if that is possible, all of quite regular habits, of acknowledged probity, with good sense, informed, all assigned to posts none of which would be more important or more honorable than another, although, because that would be impossible, they would be assigned to a less troublesome and more brilliant post when, at the end of a certain number of years, they had honorably discharged the original one."[185]

For Bolívar, the educator must be "not a sage, but indeed a man distinguished by his education, by the purity of his habits, by the naturalness of his manners, jovial, approachable, easy to get along with, frank, in short, one in whom much may be found to imitate and little to correct." This definition of the teacher establishes the ideal type of the leader of youth. But it ought not be thought that ignorance is a desirable quality in the teacher, and this cannot have been the idea of the Liberator when he asked that one choose as teacher, not a sage, but a distinguished man with purity of habits. All modern thinkers on education agree with the idea that, more than knowledge, the moral condition, the type of man he is, his quality as a person, is of fundamental value in the teacher, and this is clearly defined in the idea expressed by Bolívar.[186]

What were the functions of this teacher? Bolívar indicated what they were to be, saying, "to shape the spirit and the heart of the young . . . When prudence and skill come together to engrave the cardinal principles of virtue and honor on the souls of children, when he has managed in that way to reach their heart by means of examples and simple demonstrations that are more inspiring to watch than an emblem that is honored, than the offering of an ounce of gold, when he makes them more anxious about whether they will come to merit a reward and about feeling shame than about being deprived of the playthings and the diversions to which they are addicted, that is when he has laid the solid foundations of society; he has driven home the spur that, inspiring a noble daring in the children, they come to feel as an urge to withstand the temptations of idleness and as an impulse to devote themselves to work."

While reading the debates of the National Convention of France for the period from September 21, 1792, to May 31, 1793, I came across the ideas of the deputy Ducos, who, in a brilliant speech on the Plan of the Committee on Education, expressed conceptions quite similar to those of the Liberator. Ducos said, "If there is a function that has been made holy in the eyes of the friends of freedom it is that of the teacher in primary schools, chosen by the trust of the people to open original paths to wisdom and happiness, to create, in a certain way, a new existence for the nascent generation, which is the sweet and glorious hope of the Republic. If the difficulty of teaching finds that *it is not a greater knowledge that is necessary, but a greater exercise of reason; not a head fuller of facts and ideas, but a head better prepared for teaching to children the primary elements of science and art, for fitting to weak spirits simple and exact methods for judging things and men . . ."* (Emphasis L.B.P.) During that same time, Jean Bon Saint André said, "We lack teachers who are more concerned than instructed, more reasonable than knowledgeable."[187]

Comenius, after speaking of founding schools in every village, expressed himself in this way, "I also say that [the schools] have to be entrusted to the most respected men and women. With this observation I wish to indicate, first, that such an important thing should not be entrusted to just any person out of the mass, but only to the most select; second, that it should not be given to the young, who probably do not even know how to guide themselves."[188]

Perhaps when our Liberator wrote his own words, he was placing the whole responsibility for education in the hands of the teacher; he was thinking, more than of the lessons to be learned in the school and of what was taught in the educational establishments of the time, of the conditions that were necessary in order to train the citizen who would be capable of living in a country of men who were free and qualified to maintain and defend the freedom they had achieved: through the independence of their characters, which would never give in to flattery; through perseverance in work, which confers on each person the possession of his own destiny and relieves him of the need to fall back on others in order to maintain his dignity; and through loyalty to principles, which make each man a participant in the creation of order, in which the law shapes the conduct of each person, making him responsible for his acts.

This Bolivarian idea of the purposes of education, which guide the activities of the teacher, is coherent with all of Bolívar's social and political thought; and it indicates that the moral condition of the citizen makes him worthy of the respect of others and confers rights on him that his conduct gives back in a form that makes them invulnerable.

11. REWARDS AND PUNISHMENTS

"Moral rewards and punishments," the Liberator said, "ought to be the inducement for rational beings of a tender age; harshness and the whip is that of beasts. This system produces loftiness of spirit, nobility and dignity of feeling, decency in behavior. It contributes to an immense degree in shaping the morals of a man, creating in his inward being this invaluable treasure by virtue of which he is just, generous, human, gentle, moderate— in a word, an honorable man."

Rousseau spoke out against outrageous punishments, and before him Montaigne and Comenius had done the same. Locke held that "the usual method, the shortest and most convenient, that of punishments and the lash, which is the only instrument of governance that tutors generally know, is the least efficient of those that can be used in education."[189]

Locke's aversion to brutal acts of discipline is founded on the fact that they "do not contribute at all to dominating our natural propensity to corporal indulgence and to immediate pleasure and to evading pain at all costs; because it leads inexorably to a kind of aversion toward things, which it is the duty of the teacher to get the student to love," and "in short, because a servile discipline forms servile characters."[190]

This idea of Locke's is in agreement with that of the Liberator when he presents the image of the colonial school toward which the children feel aversion. "To say to a child, 'Let's go to school, or to see the teacher,'" Bolívar stated, "was the same as saying to him, 'Let's go to prison or to the enemy.' To take him to school and to make of him a despicable slave of fear and tedium was all one." The teachers in those schools are described by Bolívar as "ordinary men who, armed with a whip, a sullen frown, and a perpetual declamation, presented more the image of Pluto than that of a benign philosopher." In a school like that, continued the Liberator, "they teach more prejudices than truths: it is a school of servile spirits, where, along with other vices, dissimulation and hypocrisy are taught, and where fear does not permit the heart the pleasure of other sensations. Out with such tyrants! Pack them off to Salamanca, for there they would be at home."[191]

However, the thought of Locke differs from that of Bolívar since Locke does allow the use of the whip and of corporal punishment in case of obstinacy and rebellion to lazy and indifferent children when softness and moderation fail with them, after making a thorough attempt to draw them toward work and study.[192] Bolívar, on the contrary, since he is interested in the creation of a free society and in the shaping of the conscience of the Americans for the exercise of liberty, thought inapplicable at all times any educational formula that would diminish or even impede the expression of the personality that characterizes the good citizen in a free nation. For this reason he said, "a man of genius who knows the human heart and who skillfully guides a simple system and a plain and natural method, are the efficient means by which a society ought to make extraordinary and brilliant progress in a brief span of time. Without these requisites, precepts and labors will be piled up in vain: everything will be constraint and confusion."[193] This insistence on the uselessness of precepts, which on several timely occasions the Liberator pointed out, is in harmony with the thought of

Seneca, who accused the school of separating itself from life and of teaching things that were not useful for anything. "We learn, not how to live, but how to dispute," stated the old Hispanic philosopher of Rome. This was the same thought that Montaigne set down in his *Essays*, when he spoke of well-formed heads in place of well-filled ones. And Comenius said the same thing in an exciting way: "He is not wise who knows many things, but he who knows useful things." Before that he had said that "precepts are thorns for the intelligence, because they require a lot of attention and effort; on the other hand, examples offer extraordinary facility even to the most obtuse . . ."—with which he did no more than repeat the ancient dictum of Seneca, who believed that "the path of precepts is long and arduous, that of examples is short and effective."[194]

12. SOCIAL INTERCOURSE

Bolívar spoke in favor of practical instruction in the norms of behavior in society, of that which was known by the name of urbanity, which gives distinction to persons and offers a demonstration of their civility and breeding through how they behave toward those among whom they find themselves gathered. He believed that "this subject is not frivolous; its importance is such that out of its nonobservance dislikes, enmities, and duels may originate. There are persons so fine and delicate in this particular, especially foreigners, that they do not betray the slightest fault . . . The opinion of well-mannered men is that one outrages them when one falls into some irregularity in their presence." But he did speak against excessive rigidity in this teaching of the rules of urbanity and etiquette. Thus he said that "it is necessary to evade the opposite extreme, or fussy punctiliousness in the observance of the rules, from which an affectation results that is so vexatious and ridiculous that they look more like men imprinted on a few precepts than like a few precepts impressed on men."

This idea of urbanity is alien to Rousseau's thought, but it agrees with the thought of John Locke, who devotes a section of his work to the rules of behavior and sees that another, on conduct, contains all that need be known relating to behavior in society and how it may be taught. Locke also condemns harshness in dealings with tender minds, and points out that teaching by example is for them the most suitable for learning and that the passage of time is the best way of assuring that the child, in contact with persons of good manners, forgets his rusticity and adopts the ways that are permitted or advised by good society.[195]

13. HEALTH CARE

Bolívar does not forget, in his recommendations on the functioning of the public school, that it is important to incorporate within the activities of the nation those concerns that are related to health and hygiene. He thought of cleanliness, and everything referring to the healthful orientation of their life at school, as the first maxim that ought to be inculcated in children. In this part of his program, it is certain that he took his inspiration from the ideas and recommendations prescribed by Locke in his thoughts about education, since Locke, while not a doctor, showed himself to be exacting in relation to the practices that ought to be observed in order to preserve the body and the spirit in a state of health.

14. THE CONCEPT OF DISCIPLINE

In the writings we are studying an idea appears that cannot be let pass without commentary, since it would seem to be in opposition to the principles analyzed heretofore and to the kind of friendly school guided by a director whose characteristics we have previously been concerned with. Bolívar states that "teaching is only, if we might speak in this way, the disciplining of a

body of soldiers, with the difference that the soldiers are being
disciplined physically while the children are being disciplined
both physically and morally. But just as soldiers are being instructed from the time they get up in the morning until they go
to bed at night, giving regularity, time, order, and duration to all
their movements and labors in order that complete unity may
result, so the child ought to be instructed by following him
through all the hours of the day."

The strict identification of the school with a body of troops
might seem to provide the basis for equating the director with
the commandant who carries out acts of discipline in which the
recommendations made by the Liberator with respect to education are not always taken into account. However, it seems to
me that this identification is more formal than real and that
Bolívar, accustomed to the disciplined life of the army, had made
use of his great talents as an educator in order to convert the
ignorant mountaineers and the uncivilized plainsmen of our
country into a disciplined army that won independence for a
whole continent in incessant battle. The same care he recommends be applied to education he brought into play in disciplining the soldiers during the day and at night until he had created
in them the consciousness of their responsibility.

In another section I have analyzed this educational devotion
through which Bolívar shaped the conscience of his soldiers. For
him the army was, in reality, a school of human solidarity, a school
of apprenticeship in the disciplines required for service, a school
of constant sacrifice, and his educational mission was expressed
in an extraordinary way as he built this great school, to which
he dedicated all his thoughts and actions, prescribing devotion and labor for its most efficient leadership and dictating
orders that seem meticulous if one does not know the character
of the country and times in which it fell to him to act, the circumstances and the men among whom he moved, who, because they
expected everything from him, many times obstructed the action or took twisting trails to bring about the common purpose of
national liberation. As token of that generous spirit, of this attitude before men, and of the care he took in handling and in
leading them, note this paragraph in which he points out how, in
the Plains, he has to pay attention to the groups of combatants
in that region: "The columns ought not to walk much, but only

three, four, or five leagues a day, taking a siesta in a forest or beside a river from two to four in the afternoon. During this stop they ought to prepare their food. At dawn they will march two or three hours and during the late afternoon a similar number. Limes should be carried in the food stores so that they may drink limeade with brown sugar or honey—all this in order to avoid the bad climate and the excessive heat of the day and of the country."[196]

O'Leary, referring to the way Bolívar lived among the plainsmen in order to raise their morale, says, "Generals, commanders, and officers, with respect to manner of living, were on an equal footing even with the common soldier; they participated in the same details, ate the same rations, drank the same water. Even including uniforms all were equal, so that even the Liberator did not wear on the Plains any distinctive uniform. And there were even times when he was short of clothing." In this school of dignity, of democratic equality, of the glorification of human values, our people learned. Thus, the identification that the Liberator wishes to make with the school he proposes for the children of the nation.

The idea that "the child ought to be instructed by following him through all the hours of the day" expresses the modern notion that education lasts forever, from birth to death, and that at every opportunity we are learning something from life, from the persons who surround us, and from the circumstances within which we move. Modern psychology has discovered that even in dreams one is learning, and prescriptions for the teaching of languages during the hours of sleep and for influencing the mind toward the carrying out of determined activities or toward the formation of habits through the use of mechanical devices are already being put into practice. Education is a continuous process; thus, Bolívar's idea that the child ought to be followed throughout all the hours of the day has applications at the present time, and the prescription that the environment in which the child lives has to be prepared and the persons with whom he lives selected are other such educational suggestions implicit in that thought of Bolívar.

15. THE PRACTICE OF CITIZENSHIP AND CIVILITY

Finally the Liberator speaks of the division of the academy or society into three classes, in accordance with the level of training of the students. At the head of each class an inspector will be placed, freely elected from among the children themselves, distinguished by an emblem in order to stimulate the desire to occupy a post of honor among the other members of the society. This inspector is related to the monitors of the Lancasterian school. The difference is found in the way he is to be selected, which Bolívar, in order to encourage the democratic spirit, proposes be by election of the students themselves.

The Liberator recommends that "the children become accustomed to proceeding to the elections with such order and impartiality as will familiarize them with decency and justice, seeking only merit." This way of influencing the students is related to the practices of autonomous education, which provides for the organization of republics of students, sometimes in a minor imitation of governmental bodies, in order to educate the child in the observances of citizenship and to create in him the ideas of self-direction and self-discipline that are practiced in modern schools. Contained in Bolívar's proposal on the way of carrying out the elections among the students is, undoubtedly, the recognition of the importance of the democratic process of free selection of those who are to lead and to command, and of the necessity of providing, beginning in the schools, training in the sense of responsibility that provides the basis for the exercise of democracy, for those who elect as well as for those who are elected. What is important is service, and those who are designated to perform it must be conscious of their functions, and those who elect, of the respect and consideration they owe, as well as of the collaboration which they are obligated to give to those who have been elected.

This idea of encouraging the process of election beginning with the schools was to be directed toward building the road to a democratic life, which was quite precarious at the time the Liberator was writing, for which reason the very same system of elections which he established in the constitutions he wrote for Venezuela and Bolivia prescribed an elementary system of selection, which he came to think of as temporary, while apprenticeship in the civil exercise of public life was being realized. Do not forget that in the Manifesto of Cartagena, directed to the inhabitants of New Granada, the Liberator criticized the electoral system, supported by the First Republic. "Popular elections," said Bolívar, "held among the peasants of the countryside and among the scheming dwellers of the cities, add one more obstacle in the way of carrying out federation among us, because the first are so ignorant that they vote mechanically and the others are so ambitious that they convert everything into a struggle of factions; and that is why a free and equitable election has never been seen in Venezuela."[197]

The observance of elections by children in school, taking into account justice alone and seeking only merit, implied a civic training of the first order that might be diffused from the schools and, when it had come to be widespread, might effectively contribute toward creating a true idea of the act of election, which is selection among the best.

The Bolivarian system of public schools carried with it adequate incentives that, correctly applied, ought to have contributed to the improvement of the educational process.

16. "TEACHER OF PATRIOTISM"

"The winning of awards," said Bolívar, "extraordinary acts of application, of honor, and of all other noble sentiments, are not erased by forgetfulness, but rather urge themselves on the memory as tokens of self-esteem. To this end a registry will be kept, where the most notable deeds will be recorded, with the names of those who achieved them and the dates on which they occurred. It will be under the custody of a Secretary elected by vote, who will write about and approve each deed. The book will be adorned and will be maintained with veneration in a visible place. Days of great patriotic festivity will be celebrated by the society, with some notable persons of the nation as guests. One of these, the most honored, will read out loud about the glories and triumphs of the young. This ceremony will be consecrated, and acclamations and eulogies will be rendered, to those whose names are found written in this precious book. This day will be for the society a day of festivity and rejoicing."

Pedagogues of modern times and some of those from ancient times have spoken against a system of praise that could create spirits full of vanity or presumption placed above the other members of the student community. Above all, the system of giving medals in order to splatter the breast of the students like generals returning from the battlefield has come to be criticized. But the Liberator did not arrive at these celebrations with objectives that are the concern of such criticisms; he limited himself to proposing the display of the merits of those who stand out in the student society, registering them in a special book so that they might be made known to future generations of students and for the purpose too, in the same way, of recommending those who have distinguished themselves to the consideration of the larger society which they will very soon have to join.

A registry of this kind is now kept in all schools, and the system of grades as a way of measuring the learning and the conduct of the students has today a growing importance, because with it the output of the student is evaluated and the students are given opportunities to measure themselves and to surpass themselves in their own capacities. However, the system of publicity has been banished because, if it makes the better one proud, it depresses and even can nullify those with less outstanding qualities. The modern system holds that each one gives the output that his personality permits him. Merit does not rest on the fact that a person with outstanding qualities obtains extraordinary grades, but on the fact that a person of mediocre, or less than mediocre, intellectual aptitude, by an effort of excelling himself, may come to achieve a distinguished place. However, by virtue of that identification that the Liberator made between the school and the army or, better, the organizations of soldiers, by decree on October 22, 1813, he established for the courageous leaders of the Venezuelan Revolution the *Order of the Libera-*

tors, designated to "accord to the liberators of the nation an honor that distinguishes them from all others in order to express, in symbols that declare their great services, the gratitude and appreciation that everybody owes to them."

Mancini points out in a brilliant way the educational mission that inspired Bolívar when faced with undisciplined men who, without consciousness of unity in the labor of emancipation, endangered the success of the revolution with their dissensions and their dissidences, and he shows how Bolívar took on before his fellow citizens the task of "teacher of patriotism." The French biographer of our Liberator shows that "the indispensable condition for the realization, for the viability of that new work, is, however, to make of those chiefs, of those soldiers, in whose restless soul the general elements of a future nation, if one might say it like this, had taken refuge, conscious and disciplined participants in his work. They will have come to the realization of the need for altruistic abnegation; it is necessary that only the thought of having worked, of having suffered for the good of all, animate them and serve them as recompense; it is requisite, in short, that, in their turn, the masses assimilate these generous ideas and make themselves worthy of the inheritance that their liberators are preparing for them."[198]

Bolívar's constant sermons possessed the accent and the value of lessons spoken before the hearers in order to teach them the sense and the range of the nation. Between two battles, without resting, according to what we are told by this same Mancini, Bolívar "called the notables together, instructed them, explained to them what the nation had to be whose organism he was proposing to construct. His speeches, very well thought out, are true courses in public law. Made fanatic by the Liberator's proclamations and by his vehement calls to action, the people have no other ambition than that of enlisting in the ranks of the republican army, which grows hour by hour."[199]

For his great school of patriotism, as for the public schools planned by him, Bolívar creates incentives that are intended to elevate merit and to make it possible for the great work of any man to be considered by his fellow citizens and to merit the recognition and respect of all.

17. THE EDUCATIONAL VALUE
OF ERROR

I have noted in another place that in all of Bolívar's acts and in his public and private writings, ideas or attitudes constantly appear that tend to create in his fellow citizens a kind of behavior that would redound to the benefit of the national community, in short, a form of conduct that would reveal the effect of an educative activity. In a letter to General José de Sucre, in which he warns against a possible change of tactics on the part of the defeated Spanish armies, he says that those armies even after having failed could be expected to act in a way that would favor their own interests, because "things, in order that they be done well, have to be done twice . . . the first time instructs the second."

This phrase, taken in isolation, would be simply the repetition of statements made by thinkers and educators all through history. Comenius said, "What has to be done should be learned doing it."[200] Action conduces to learning, and errors teach how to correct the path of failure. This is what is called in modern educational psychology the method of trial and error, in which failures are corrected and successes are reinforced, in order to arrive at an adequate form of behavior. Domingo F. Sarmiento, President of Argentina in the middle of the last century, whose concern with educational activity was also extensive, will say that things have to be done badly, but done; later on, the adjustments will come. Rousseau too spoke of the need for allowing the child his own experience, without attaching any importance to the mistakes he makes, for later on the corrections would be bound to come.[201]

But the important thing is that the sense in which and the occasion on which these words were spoken by Bolívar constitute a lesson intended to alert his student, who had a predilection for trusting in the persistence of the enemy's error. Bolívar was to such an extent right in his predictions that, on account of not considering these forecasts of what was to happen, the army of

Peru was almost destroyed by those who, having made a mistake, learned in that error the way of rectifying it in order to achieve success.

18. AN ENDURING EDUCATIONAL
MISSION

There are in the communications of the Liberator to Sucre, to Heres, to Briceño Méndez, to Santander, and to others of his correspondents a series of ideas, of educational thoughts, that if they were ever to be analyzed would reveal a whole system of ideas for action and a cloud of teachings that this "teacher of patriotism" continued to sow in the consciousnesses of his followers in order to create the exemplary virtues of the people and of their leaders in America. He had a clear consciousness of what his own example meant, for in him the spirit of the educator was very much alive. To his nephew Anacleto Clemente, who was carrying on a life of dissipation in Bogotá, he wrote, "Does it not make you ashamed to see that some poor men out of the plains, without education, without the means of obtaining it, who have never had any other school but a guerrilla band, have made themselves into gentlemen, have converted themselves into men of honor, have learned to respect themselves only because of my respecting myself? Does it not make you ashamed, I repeat, to consider that, as you are my nephew, as you have for mother a woman of the most rigorous morals, you are inferior to many a poor warrior who has no family but his homeland?"[202] This reproach directed to his scatterbrained nephew gives proof of the clear notion of this educational influence on men of humble origins, who through his example raised themselves to the majesty of the citizen, and proves as well that, more than blood, what is important is the exemplary attitude and the leadership of a great teacher and the whole will placed into service.

To this educative capacity of Bolívar, O'Leary alludes when, in the biographical sketch he drew of him, he said, "[Bolívar] had the gift of persuasion and knew how to inspire confidence in others. To those qualities are due, in great part, the astounding triumphs that he obtained in such difficult circumstances; because any other man, without these gifts and without his decisiveness of soul, would have been discouraged. A creative genius par excellence, he drew resources out of nothing." That is the essence of his great and imponderable educational influence, which was devoted wholly to the creation of the consciousness of a nation. That is why one of his biographers, the German writer Gerhard Masur, says that "along the course of his life his task was to breathe a spirit in the clay of American existence, and his many proclamations and summonses ought to be judged in this sense. They were not born in the beginning out of a desire to show himself off brilliantly or for his own glorification, but rather they had the intention of inculcating in the apathetic masses a national and continental consciousness. Only Bolívar could have stirred them out of their dreams and guided them into an active life."[203]

Indeed, to awaken the men of our continent in order to assign them actively to the task of creation constitutes the essence of the thought and of the militant educational labors of Simón Bolívar. His final words from the Hacienda de San Pedro Alejandrino, in which he calls for unity against anarchy, are related to his first words from the Patriotic Society on July 4, 1811. In those earlier words he was calling for the effort to win the freedom of a continent, and in his last words for the preservation of that freedom —freedom that had been won by the iron lasso of the unity of the spirit and of the peoples, who are always in danger of falling into slavery if they are not ready, vigilant, to block the growth of the forces of dissolution, a permanent menace to harmonious democratic life, which has its basis in mutual respect, in shared tasks, in loyalty to the institutions and uncorruptible adherence to the law considered as the rule of contention and the boundary of one's own rights as well as of the rights of others.

The educational mission of Simón Bolívar is permanent, just as the example of his life and his fervent devotion to serving us is enduring—rousing in us too a passion for service and love of country, virtues that are not always shared or jealously guarded, but which are the imperatives indicated by the voice of our great guide, teacher of effort, in whom the active example was always related to the instructive word.

Appendix

TWO SPEECHES ON BOLÍVAR

THE RELEVANCE OF BOLÍVAR

An address delivered on September 6, 1961, in Tegucigalpa, Republic of Honduras, on the occasion of the unveiling there of a statue of the Liberator, donated by the government of Venezuela. Dr. Prieto presided over the Venezuelan delegation in attendance at this ceremony.

We have come to plant in the homeland of Francisco Morazán a bountiful tree, which, while it has its expression in this equestrian statue of our Liberator, will lavishly grow protective branches and put forth seeds in abundance that the winds of democracy will bring to flower perennially. We are performing here a ritual of sowers; the seed put into the furrow, but hope placed in a future of prodigious harvests—and this is because we, Venezuelans, Americans, cannot look upon Bolívar simply as a historical figure who realized a task, but as a seed of thought, growing, flowering, and bearing fruit forever. For Bolívar's thought renews itself every day, just as planting and harvest are new in the newly cultivated lands of this America of ours, and the pain of sowing it and the sweat of cultivating it and the love of harvesting it is the mature fruit, the labor of all the generations of Americans who believe in freedom as the food of the soul for those who love democracy as an equalizing way of life and who are determined to live in peace, so that the estate we conquer may serve the people without diminution of rights and in the plenitude of the duties that pertain to all.

Bolívar and continental solidarity. The ideas of Bolívar have a content that transcends his time and his land, for he thought with his vision set on the future. He dreamed of one America, united in the effort to conquer freedoms, and united too for the progress and well-being of its peoples. When in 1818, surrounded by enemies, in the midst of effervescent countries, he wrote to the Director of the United Provinces of Río de la Plata, Don Juan Martín de Pueyrredón, about the necessity of establishing an "American pact that, forming from all our republics one political body, would introduce America to the world with an appearance of majesty and greatness that has no model in the nations of antiquity," he laid the foundations of continental solidarity and affirmed the ideals that are now being accepted in spite of the barriers of misunderstandings in the world as a whole. He was the artificer of the ideas that are giving shape to a united America. He tried to put an end to the disputes over boundaries and to internal quarrels, thinking toward the common destiny that the future will have to offer us, in order that a united America may be called "Queen of Nations and Mother of Republics."

Bolívar, always relevant. Bolívar is relevant at all times. As our nations struggle to get out of the backwardness in which they have come to be submerged and which was pointed out by Bolívar in his famous "Jamaican Letter," a letter that is now 146 years old, we find inspiration for the work of progress that we need, for the planning of constructive activity, for the utilization of natural resources, which belong to the people, for the benefit of the people, because, as I have said elsewhere, what is great and marvelous in Bolívar is that he has a solution adequate to every circumstance.

That prolific way of proceeding placed him at the center of activity in a turbulent world. In him, the human quality, the capacity for leadership, reached dimensions of excellence, converting him into the exemplar and model for a continent. I will repeat here what I have said elsewhere: Bolívar's action was more than a liberating action, more than a freeing action, because he devoted himself to teaching men the use of that recently achieved liberty and how to restrain the abuses and excesses of those who, since they are not accustomed to acting freely, run the risk of getting lost along the way. In him, in addition to the great commander and leader of armies, one has to see the leader of peoples who, surpassing himself in the fight against adversity and against oppression, becomes a people too in order to find in the formless clay of the anonymous mass inspiration for his work of redemption.

Bolívar thought that "an ignorant people is the blind instrument of its own destruction," but his words have to be interpreted now as something more than an allusion to the illiterate men and women who were the material of the armies that, following him, went about sowing freedoms. For, it is not only ignorance of the written word that destroys our people, since educated men suffer, at times, from an ignorance that is blind to the science they never learned, the science of the heart and feelings. That is why, while humble and illiterate people work the earth, tend the cattle, and die in abandonment, others enjoy in tranquil leisure the learning that makes them insensitive and the riches that separate them from misery.

Land for the Indians. The Bolívar we are planting in these lands of Central America is the human Bolívar, who promotes agrarian reform, giving his own lands to the soldiers who joined the ranks of the liberating army, who wrote the law of land distribution of 1819, who in 1825, from the city of Cuzco, proclaimed: "It is declared that the Indians are the owners of the land they occupy. The communal lands are to be divided among the Indians who do not have any land of their own. The distribution will be accomplished taking into account the condition of each recipient, assigning more lands to the heads of families, but in such a way that no Indian is left without his own plot of land."

The problem of the land, which we have been dragging behind us since the earliest days of the conquest, when the Indians were consigned to the great lords, for whom they cultivated the immense estates that were conferred on the Spaniards by the King, grew worse day by day until it came to constitute the basis for an iniquitous exploitation of the peasants in our America. The whole of America has been a continent of great landed estates, unproductive at times, but always the expression of an attitude of aggrandizement on the part of men whose power depended on the ready use of the gallows and the knife, who were able to control immense territories where they enslaved the people already established in them.

Agrarian reform was converted, for that reason, into a necessity; and Bolívar saw clearly that in order to free the Indian and the American peasant it was not enough to promise them political rights without at the same time placing them in conditions where they could take care of themselves on their own by obtaining subsistence for their families from their own land. *Bread, land, and liberty* was the cry smothered in the throats of our oppressed peoples, who, as they ran after the cavalry of the liberators, felt that the homeland was wherever they could live peacefully in the warmth of a home of their own, which would grow and be maintained by the independent efforts of its members. The nation that the Liberator taught love for was not that declaimed in the verses of the poets, nor in high-sounding speeches, not that which was sung about in anthems, but a nation that has its roots in American reality, in the problems of the people, in bonds of solidarity that are firmly united for the purpose of seeking contentment in labor—and nothing can hold a man more securely in that universal feeling for country than the sense of security that is offered by his own land and his own labor. In order to create that sense of country and the emotional attachments that accompany it, Bolívar assumed the terrible responsibility of separating the dominated from those who dominated them, teaching the former how to conquer their right to live and marking the latter for punishment on account of the depredation to which they had condemned the defenseless beings who served them.

In Bolívar agrarian reform has a predecessor with great prestige; and when the peoples of America express the desire to carry out that reform in multilateral accords, Bolívar's thought, which is an inexhaustible source of inspiration for the work of redemption of our peoples, will come back into its own.

Several countries of our America—Mexico first, Bolivia, Cuba, Guatemala, Venezuela, in different ways and attending to different realities—have sought to put the land into the hands of those who work it; all have understood that to distribute the land is to distribute wealth, with the aim of making each man more master of himself, but that possession of land is conditioned by the will to make it produce, not only for one's own benefit, but for the benefit of the entire community. To redistribute the land, unless there is at the same time concern for its rational utilization, can be a useless expedient, similar to that of distributing pieces of paper without value on which the monetary symbols of a nonexistent wealth are represented.

The American nations, meeting at the recent Conference of Punta del Este in Uruguay, voted to carry out agrarian reform in all our countries, and it was specifically Venezuela, making itself the advocate of the thought of Bolívar, that tried to pay homage to his initiative at the moment of celebrating the hundred fiftieth anniversary of American Independence. It was an unfulfilled obligation, which had been assumed in the Laws of Land Distribution, promulgated when the blood of the liberating armies was still running over the soil of our country, making it fertile. Venezuela had begun to fulfill its promise of carrying out agrarian reform. On March 5 last year, in Campo de Carabobo, the Venezuelan Agrarian Law was promulgated. Those who died for our liberty on that field of battle, the plainsmen of General Páez, the men of the Andes, the men of the coastal regions—all those who were gathered there, without distinction of class, were inspired by the purpose that guided Bolívar to create a system of human community that would produce justice, and the immediate children of his thought were making themselves ready to make good his promise when Venezuela again took the path of democracy and when its people are the masters of their destiny. To political democracy we have added economic democracy, in the social formula in which it is provided that "nobody shall have too much and nobody too little."

The agreements on mutual assistance and co-operation between the American states, the charter of the Alliance for Progress, signed at Punta del Este, interpret the desires of an America united as one nation, but not for the sake of a vaunting exhibition of external sovereignty, always precarious, but for the sake of the authentic enjoyment of internal security and liberty, with the co-operation and respect of all the peoples of the world. Peaceful effort is beginning to materialize, through the associative purpose of turning progress into the inheritance of humanity, each one contributing in the measure of his capacities and possibilities the support that is necessary, the rich nations and powers their resources, the poor ones their labor. Only in this way will there be peace among our peoples, each one master of the estate it cultivates, master of its destiny as a people, master, in short, of the immense patrimony of endeavors with the aim that there no longer be either exploited or exploiters.

Bolívar and world peace. The people of this America of ours possess the right to the full enjoyment of their social, political, and economic liberty, to contentment free of worries, without the fear of armed aggressions coming from the outside and without the threat of despotic regimes implanted on the inside for the perpetuation of inequality and injustice.

The restlessness of life in the world that is now being experienced makes survival almost impossible, since "while the villager in his shack is inventing new life, in the laboratory the man of science is inventing new death"—as our poet Andrés Eloy Blanco would say. Today the world is tired of being threatened by a bomb from which there is no shelter, and humanity, imprisoned in fear, no longer knows the humble labor of making bread for the daily ration consumed in peace, because mixed into the mass of dough are worries about surmounting the uncertain life that the poor are suffering, while for the rich there is no escaping dangers that threaten everybody.

If the money invested by powerful nations in the manufacture of powerful destructive devices were employed in an alliance for progress, misery would rapidly disappear from the face of the earth, and with it unrest and injustice, and these nations of the Isthmus would become, as Bolívar dreamed of their being, "the trading center of the world."

Here, Bolívar thought, is the center of America, which could very well be the location for the capital of the world—except that it would not be good for us to dream of being a target for the wanton destructiveness of which the powers of our time are possessed. We will satisfy ourselves with being left to live in peace, working together to achieve economic independence together, through the promotion of an autonomous development that will put the natural resources at the service of the people of our continent and make of science and culture the common wealth of all.

Bolívar's thought as a seed. Bolívar is the guide. His thought, the seed sown here, will go on bearing fruit, and our primary needs, which are, as he said, morality and enlightenment, will go on being propagated, but only to the degree that the cultivated land, the productive factory, and swift transportation make possible the passage of wealth and effort, and only when our peoples have brought their sovereignty into force and made it prevail in order to free it from external assault and internal appropriation. Only when we have made the democratic way of life effective and permanent, with all it implies of tolerance and understanding, work in common, division of responsibility, in short, justice and living together in harmony. Only when the will to power of men and of groups is no longer raised as a threat to break the law and to push constitutions aside, setting up the will of a soldier of fortune above the general will—for, as Bolívar said, "A fortunate soldier has no right to rule his country. He is not the judge of its laws or of government; he is the defender of its freedom." Within an authentic democracy nobody has the right to set aside the sovereignty of the people.

We are met together around the statue of Bolívar, young people and old, men and women, soldiers and civilians, not in order to comply with a fleeting ritual, but in order to dedicate ourselves to the purpose of doing justice so that we may be true to ourselves, because for Bolívar "justice is the queen of republican virtues, and with it equality and liberty are sustained," the purpose of devotion and sacrifice for the good of our fellow citizens, because "he who gives up everything in order to be useful to his country, does not lose anything, but rather gains whatever he bestows."

We aspire to the glory that will give greatness to America, which will be our greatness, possible only, in accordance with the doctrine of Bolívar, to the degree that we become most useful.

In the land of Morazán and De Valle, the seed of Bolívar is already sown. Its fruits are the fruits of liberty and democracy, which are obtained only through the irrigation of the constant efforts that the people themselves bestow. I am acquainted with the men and women of this people, for I have lived among their sorrows and their joys, and for this reason I know them to be capable of making this bountiful tree grow and bear fruit. That our labor as sowers be prodigal in the harvest of successes is the most fervent wish of the government and of the people of Venezuela, whom it has been my honor to represent in this ceremony, which is a celebration of solidarity, of recognition, and of understanding.

BOLÍVAR AND AGRARIAN REFORM

Opening address delivered at the unveiling ceremony of an equestrian statue of the Liberator, Simón Bolívar, in the plaza named after him in Turén, Venezuela, on December 29, 1963.

The return of Bolívar. In this rural town of Turén, close to the foot of the range of the Andes, when the plains begin and the mountains end, well it is that here the Father of the Nation brings his glorious turbulence to a quiet flowing. He came across the mountains, breaking down the underbrush; he passed through the cities, he was pained more by the spirit, the moral misery, than by the misery of the body. More than a hundred fifty years after he chose for his career the pursuit of liberty, in that admirable gesture that brought him the name of Liberator, he was still looking for friendly simplicity in the peace of the countryside, which gave him so much pleasure as a child.

Here, raised by the people in a joyous effort, his figure grew, metal in a flaming fire for eternity. Smelted by the expert hand of the Venezuelans, in collaboration with Italian artists, now he is raised, not in the motionless gesture of the statue alone, but in that of the example that flows from his life, when in order to speak his words for the centuries he passes among the workers of the land and in an openhearted way invites them to labor, when in order to state his faith in the future of our nation he summons them to continue the struggle to strengthen civil life, protected by the laws and by the institutions that these laws had built, and the conquests achieved with pain and with blood on the fields of battle.

It is no longer the general of ardent speech, praising the courage of those who kill, but the man of peace, the civil Bolívar, who has left the encampment and finds that his people, who came from the ranks of the liberating army, are working the land, guarding the cattle, and in the warmth of their homes are forging a new and independent life, which is not to be achieved except in satisfying labor, when freedom allows each one to win his

livelihood without loss of dignity and to live from the effort that
waters his own furrow with his own sweat, without fear of losing
what has been gained but also without ambition of taking from
others what belongs to them by virtue of the work they have
expended to achieve it.

The Liberator arrived at this town at a favorable time, when
the streak of despotism had already passed that made of its
land a place of slavery and misery; but those who came after
him turned their backs on his command and instead of working
for the humble dedicated themselves to forging new chains and
to making more unhappy their passage through the earth. He
comes at a good time, because the democracy that he dreamed
about for his people, so many times lost, so many times regained,
is already growing, within a forest of free spirits, and now
definitely exists, in firm permanence upon Venezuelan soil, because the people learned from his words that only that man
is worthy of freedom who is capable of conquering it and who
has enough uprightness of will to maintain it, exalt it, and defend it.

The history of Venezuela has been crossed by marches and
countermarches in search of freedom, and it was always Bolívar, since the days of independence, who has been invoked by
some in order to impose their will and by others to affirm their
right to live with dignity and to dream of a future without appre-
hension. Arc of alliance for some, destructive battering ram in
the hands of those who, calling themselves interpreters of his
thought, disavowed him a thousand times and a thousand
times prostituted what he represents for Venezuela. Fortunately
now he grows, his prestige vindicated, through the thought that
he left us and through the faith that has taken root among the
humble people who, in spite of the avatars of our history,
dreamed that someday, breaking down the mountains and passing through cities, just as they had a hundred fifty years ago, they
would carry forth the inspiration so that their children might take
the path that he had pointed out when the nation was hardly
more than an aspiration of a few and the determined pledge
of his liberating will.

An occasion of affirmation of the will of Venezuela has just
been completed, and one government risen out of the popular
will, freely expressed, is being followed by another chosen by

the people in free elections, and in this way, from hand to hand, the right to rule the fortunes of the nation will have to be transmitted in the future, because the people want it this way, in spite of those who think that the judgment of the people is not justice, which is what Dr. José María Vargas would have said, but that justice lives by the kind of force that the would-be assassin Pedro Carujo decided upon. Here an expression of Bolívar's is relevant, that expression in which, trying to restrain the ambitions of his fellow officers and to point out a path for those who would command the army, he said, "A fortunate soldier has no right to rule his country. He is not the arbiter of its laws, nor of government; he is the defender of its freedom." His words are relevant too when he places justice above victory, thinking as he was of all those who had been living starved for justice: the peasants who had not received equal treatment, the humble men who worked in the factories, and those who, having nothing, were treated and mistreated by those raised to pre-eminence in fortune and to the power that this pre-eminence offers.

Agrarian reform. Venezuela has begun to do justice and along with that to realize the equality of Venezuelans, not only before the law, which can be a deceptive way of making equality sacred, when in order to get one's rights one needs money in order to make the organisms charged with administering that justice work, but in social justice, which puts into the hands of the state the obligation of helping and, on a preferential basis, taking care of those in need, without, however, establishing differences between one Venezuelan and another, since all are worthy of equal treatment.

The justice that is being done in Venezuela had its beginnings with the fulfillment of a promise made by the Liberator in 1817, when he ordered that the lands confiscated from the partisans of the King be divided among the men who had conquered freedom, who were no other than the people in arms, who had followed Boves because he had promised them land, money, saddles, and horses, and who later transferred their impulsiveness to the ranks of the lancers who spurred their horses under the leadership of Páez, because he had, in 1816, promised to divide among the soldiers of Apure the wealth belonging to the government. Bolívar's promise, signed into law with the Law of Land Distribution, was converted into paper money of the public debt, which hungry soldiers sold for five per cent of their value, so that they went on without lands, while these lands were cornered by a few generals with a fortune in money and by businessmen taking advantage of the misery of the soldiers of freedom.

Bolívar, a rich landowner, perhaps one of the richest of all Venezuelans in landed property, thought that such disproportionate possession was an injustice, for it meant that the people generally lacked even a parcel of land for their own cultivation, and he proposed that the land belong to whoever worked it. Agrarian reform, which was intended to make the peasants who lived from the land free, was a part of the cluster of Bolívar's thoughts, of his eagerness to complete political independence with economic freedom. What is currently called agrarian democracy Bolívar understood as an exemplary form of his liberating action. For that reason, he believed that the peasants who made up the army, "the soldiers of the liberating army were too much worthy of the recompense of the government for it to be able to forget them. Men who have faced all dangers, who have left behind them all their wealth and goods, and who have suffered all ills, should not be left without the just reward that their dispossession, their courage, and their virtue merit." But, once the war was over, when the bonds representing lands had been sold, and, in spite of the Liberator's protests, the men who in Congress and in the administration were entrusted with putting Bolívar's thought into practice thwarted his intentions, then the peasants, who returned from combat covered with wounds and with glory, were to know of the land only so much as would cover the length of their bodies.

Bolívar's thought on agrarian reform has now begun to be put into practice. He thought in 1825 at Cuzco that "the Indians ought to be the owners of the land they occupy. The communal lands ought to be divided among those who do not have any land of their own, taking into account the condition of each recipient, but in such a way that no Indian is left without his own plot of land." In Venezuela, as well as in Colombia, in Ecuador, in Peru, and in Bolivia, the nations born out of his liberating toil, Bolívar's ideas on agrarian reform had been pushed to one side, but the hour of justice is coming, and first in Bolivia, later in

Venezuela, and now in Peru, the promise of land for the peasant is being made into a reality.

The peasants of Turén, in prosperous cultivation of their own land, are witnesses to the reality of this thought of Bolívar's, and when they plant it in their fields, in the statue that watches over their sowing, they are also testifying to their will to maintain the conquest that has been won and to see to it not only that the land produces sustenance for the country family but that it contributes, as a common good, to improve the conditions of life for all the people, who in a permanent interchange of products give the peasant the possibilities of acquiring goods produced in the factory in exchange for the products that are in excess from his bountiful harvest.

These lands of the state of Portuguesa, all the high plains, where the rivers cross one another and are no longer a dangerous menace, because dams like the one at Las Majaguas and that at Masparro are being placed across the riotous fury of their waters, in order to convert them into a source of irrigation—all these lands are a trading center of wealth for the whole of Venezuela. Here and in Barinas and Cojedes, effort grows into works, and the plains are already rid of that terrible disease, malaria; the human current that previously used to go from the savannah to the mountains now takes the reverse route; and men without land in the high Andean plateaus are populating the plains for a new and better humanity, in a thorough integration of country Venezuela, which is getting together to work for the economic future of the nation.

In the state of Portuguesa, agrarian reform can be heard on the march: industrious tractors are breaking new ground into furrows; as Bolívar wished, there is a diversity of crops, substituted for the traditional sowings for subsistence, so that a profusion of products are growing as raw materials for industry, sesame, cotton, tobacco, rice; and it is promised that within a short time, through the efforts of the workingmen of these lands, the sugar mill will be a reality, which, together with the already promising plantings of fruit trees, will contribute to increasing the personal wealth of the peasant in a more just distribution of the national product, with incalculable benefits for the entire nation.

The love of the law. Now, after having achieved the reform that gives the land to the peasant and provides credit and technical assistance, at a time when the anguish of the people is already beginning to diminish, since we are now on the path to justice, we must maintain an alert spirit and a vigilant conscience in order not to be diverted from the direction we have chosen and in order that the law go on being the secure path for the transit of Venezuelan life, so that the thought that Bolívar expressed in the Congress of Angostura, where he attributed to Venezuelans little love for the law, ceases to be valid. The Liberator said, "Love of country, love for the law, love for government officials, are the noblest passions that ought to exclusively absorb the soul of a republican. Venezuelans love their country, but they do not love its laws; because these laws have been noxious and were the sources of evil. They have not been able to love the government officials either, because they were iniquitous, and the new ones are hardly known in the career upon which they have entered. If there is not a sacred respect for the nation, for the laws, and for the authorities, society is a confusion, a single combat of man against man, of body against body."

But the laws to which Bolívar was referring were those we inherited from the Spanish Empire, and the government officials, those who represented that oppressive empire. Now, however, the laws are born out of the popular will, and the representatives of this will are those entrusted with drawing them up, taking into account the purpose and the supreme end of the collective welfare. Government officials are no longer imposed by a foreign power; they are chosen by the whole people from among the most distinguished of its men, since they are aware of their virtues, since they know their sacrifices, since they have taken whole and exact measure of them according to how capable they are of acting for the benefit of the community. There is thus no reason why disaffection with the law and the officials should go on carrying confusion into the public life of Venezuela, making possible the enthronement of opportunistic men who make a law of their own will and impose it by force.

One's own fire and a foreign lamp. Some Venezuelans, who are without respect for their people or for their institutions, making use of force, right here in this place as well as in other zones, sheltered in the underbrush, want to bring from the forests a rustic formula for running the government, and even when they have come into the cities and drink in, at the colleges and universities, theories for the taking and holding of power, they forget the civilized formulas of peaceful struggle in order to follow the short cut of armed struggle. They are the wandering guerrillas who try to involve the peasants in their disorderly way of conceiving the change of government and of institutions, but the peasants everywhere turn their backs on them, for the peasants are desirous of winning peace and tranquillity in their homes and, after more than a hundred years of hazardous imposition of governments by force, are content to have the government that they themselves have produced, supported by their own free will and tenaciously defended so that Venezuela shall continue to be the land of liberty and so that Bolívar will no longer wear his sullen frown, which has been an enduring reproach to Venezuelans, to all Americans, who have not known how to carry out his injunctions and have given free reign to their passions, twisting the law and spiriting away free and peaceful discussion from the institutional life of our peoples.

This town of Turén, when it has been necessary to struggle for freedom, has done it with dignity and with vigor, just as it struggles by honest labor to achieve welfare. Here is an abundance of the lives of humble men who pitted their courage against the excesses of the dictatorship that was overthrown on January 23, 1958. From these fields the armies that made the Federalist War were nourished, possessed of a keenness for liberty and the desire to win the land and bread that had been promised by all the military chiefs who got the Venezuelan people to follow them. From these lands the Army of Liberation recruited the men who fought at Araure and Carabobo. Through the treeless plains of Barinas, the great state that covers this immensity of high plains, men pass setting fire to the plains, men who were seeking equality and justice by the effort of their lances and the shot of their rifles—equality and justice, the fundamental postulates put into circulation from Angostura by the Liberator in 1819.

For this reason the agitators of armed struggle will be defeated, for they urge now neither justice nor equality, for they do not fight a battle to eradicate the foreign powers of foreign domination from our soil, nor seek for the peasant the land promised by the Liberator, but, on the contrary, want to impose foreign doctrines on the people who created the doctrine of liberty for America and want to hold up as valorous heroes, whom our men are supposed to follow, those who in other lands are despotic, when we possess in Bolívar an enduring model and in the men who follow his thought, effective and valuable leaders. We do not have to light a foreign lamp when we have a fire to illuminate the skies of liberty and to create clarity of consciousness in peoples benumbed by the ignominy, the barbarity, and the slavery that are imposed upon them by their own children and by the foreign doctrine.

The unveiling of this statue of our Liberator, Simón Bolívar, the first to be cast in Venezuela itself, expresses more than homage to the hero who gave us liberty; it expresses the aim of affirming our own capacity for fulfillment, fulfilling ourselves. We do not make Bolívar in our own image and likeness in the bronze in which we have cast him, but we place there part of what he has given us, as an incorruptible seed in time, sown in good land, that seed which is the generous heart of Bolívar, so that it will go on growing in his guiding will and so that his thought, from this high plain, will go on spreading clarity and realizing in Venezuela the nation of which he dreamed, the nation of all, in the effort shared by all, in the thought cleansed of ambitions, and in the will placed wholly in the service of our people, which is the ultimate reason for the anguish we carry within us and for our devotion to Venezuela.

Notes

1. Luis B. Prieto F., *Problemas de la educación venezolana* (Caracas: Imprenta Nacional, 1947), pp. 32–34.
2. José Gil Fortoul, *Historia constitucional de Venezuela*, cuarta edición (Caracas: Ministerio de Educación, 1953), vol. I, pp. 315, 324.
3. Jules Mancini, in writing his work *Bolívar y la emancipación de las colonias españolas*, which was originally published in French (Paris: Libraire Académique, Perrin et Cie., 1912), no doubt had at hand the work of Gil Fortoul, from which he quotes (p. 32 of the Spanish edition). Mancini died in December 1912, without having had time to revise his work, and for this reason the Spanish translation that I have consulted, which is the work of Carlos Docteur (Braile Le Conve: Editorial Bouret), does not vary in any way from the original.
4. Jules Mancini, *op. cit.*, p. 151.
5. *Ibid.*, p. 324. Note the similarity of language and even the use of the same words in Gil Fortoul and Mancini.
6. Angel Rosenblatt, introduction to Martha Hildebrandt, *La lengua de Bolívar*, vol. I, *Léxico* (Caracas: Universidad Central de Venezuela, 1961), pp. 7, 8.
7. Martha Hildebrandt, *op. cit.*, pp. 97, 115.
8. *Ibid.*, p. 21.
9. Marius André, *Bolívar y la democracia* (Barcelona: Casa Editorial Araluce, 1924), chapters II and III, pp. 30 ff.
10. C. Parra Pérez, *Bolívar: Contribución al estudio de sus ideas políticas*, segunda edición (Caracas: Escuela Técnica Industrial, 1942), pp. 9–10.
11. *Ibid.*, p. 10.
12. Armando Rojas, *Ideas educativas de Simón Bolívar*, segunda edición (Caracas-Madrid: Ediciones Edime, 1955), pp. 30, 31.
13. Jean Jacques Rousseau, *Emilio*, in *Obras escogidas* (Buenos Aires: Editorial El Ateneo, 1950), p. 523.
14. *Ibid.*, p. 460.
15. Immanuel Kant, quoted by Ernst Cassirer in *Filosofía de la Ilustración*, segunda edición (Mexico: Fondo de Cultura Económica, 1950), pp. 185–86.
16. C. Parra Pérez, *op. cit.*, p. 53.
17. Joseph Lancaster, in a letter to Bolívar published in *Bolívar y su época*, Publicaciones de la Secretaría General de la Décima Conferencia Interamericana, Colección Historia, no. 10 (Caracas, 1953), vol. I, p. 14.

18. The text of these decrees may be consulted in *Revista de la Sociedad Bolivariana de Venezuela,* vol. XXII, no. 77 (December 17, 1963), published in Caracas.

19. ARMANDO ROJAS, *op. cit.,* in chapter VIII, "Bolívar y la universidad," pp. 149 ff.

20. MARISA VANNINI DE GERULEWIEZ, *La influencia francesa en Venezuela* (Maracaibo: Editorial Universidad del Zulia, 1965), p. 23.

21. Letter sent from Angostura to the "Excelentísimo Señor Supremo Director" of the United Provinces of the Río de la Plata, Juan Martín de Pueyrredón. Simón Bolívar, *Obras completas* (Havana: Editorial Lex, 1947), vol. I, pp. 293–94.

22. JOSÉ DOMINGO DÍAZ, *Recuerdos de la Rebelión de Caracas,* published on the hundred fiftieth anniversary of Venezuelan independence. (Caracas: Biblioteca de la Academia de la Historia, 1961), pp. 98–99.

23. SIMÓN BOLÍVAR, *Obras completas,* vol. II, p. 105.

24. *Ibid.,* pp. 1001–2.

25. *Ibid.,* p. 1015.

26. JOSÉ MANUEL RESTREPO, *Historia de Colombia,* vol. I, p. 313.

27. J. F. DE HEREDIA, *Memorias de Regente Heredia* (Madrid: Editorial América), pp. 205–6.

28. SIMÓN BOLÍVAR, *Obras,* vol. I, p. 191.

29. The desire to end the "war to the death," always present in Bolívar's thoughts, was clearly expressed in a letter directed to General Morillo, who was then surrounded at Calabozo. The letter speaks thus, "To the Commander of the Spanish Troops in Calabozo, Don Pablo Morillo: Our humanity, against all the demands of justice, has many times suspended the bloody war to the death that the Spaniards wage against us. For the last time, I offer the cessation of such a horrible calamity, and I begin my offer by returning all the prisoners that we took yesterday on the field of battle. May that example of generosity be the ultimate outrage to our enemies!" Simón Bolívar, *Obras,* vol. I, p. 282.

30. SIMÓN BOLÍVAR, *ibid.,* p. 1284. To Francisco de Paula Santander, who seemed to be thinking along the same lines as Páez, the Liberator wrote, dated February 21, 1826, from La Magdalena, Peru, "That plan [to put a crown on his head] offends me more than all the injuries of my enemies, since it attributes to me an ordinary ambition and an infamous soul capable of identifying itself with Iturbide and those other miserable usurpers. According to those gentlemen, nobody can be great except in the way of Alexander, Caesar, and Napoleon." And he con-

cluded, "I wish to surpass them all in disinterestedness, since I cannot equal them in greatness of deeds. My example can serve for something to my country itself, since the moderation of the chief executive will spread to the least, and my life will be their rule. The people will adore me, and I will be the safeguard of their alliance." *Ibid.*, p. 1273.

31. *Ibid.*, pp. 70–71.

32. *Ibid.*, vol. II, p. 1133.

33. *Ibid.*, p. 1178.

34. *Ibid.*, p. 1077.

35. SIMÓN BOLÍVAR, speech in the Church of St. Francis in Caracas, January 2, 1814, before the Assembly meeting there: *ibid.*, p. 1051.

36. RUFINO BLANCO-FOMBONA, *Pensamiento vivo de Bolívar* (Buenos Aires: Editorial Losada, 1944), p. 21.

37. SIMÓN BOLÍVAR, *Obras*, vol. I, p. 92.

38. *Ibid.*, p. 149.

39. *Ibid.*, p. 986.

40. *Ibid.*, p. 176.

41. *Ibid.*, pp. 176–77.

42. *Ibid.*, p. 133.

43. *Ibid.*, pp. 162–63.

44. *Ibid.*, pp. 221–22.

45. *Ibid.*, p. 73.

46. *Ibid.*, p. 74.

47. JUAN VICENTE GONZÁLEZ, as quoted by Cornelio Hispano, *Libro de Oro de Bolívar* (Paris: Casa Editora Garnier Hermanos, 1925), p. 122. In a proclamation of January 1, 1817, Bolívar had promised his companions at arms: "You will fly with me to wealthy Peru. Our destinies call us to the ends of the American world." Simón Bolívar, *Obras*.

48. Letter to Don José Manuel Restrepo from Don Joaquín Mosquera, as quoted by Cornelio Hispano, *op. cit.*, pp. 204–5.

49. RUFINO BLANCO-FOMBONA, *op. cit.*, p. 182.

50. L. PERÚ DE LACROIX, *Diario de Bucaramanga*, edited by Monsignor Nicolás E. Navarro (Caracas: Tipografía Americana, 1935), pp. 260–62.

51. SIMÓN BOLÍVAR, *Obras*, vol. I, p. 1083.

52. *Ibid.*, p. 172.

53. *Ibid.*, vol. II, pp. 1135–36.

54. SIMÓN BOLÍVAR, words spoken to Commodore Hull, quoted by Rufino Blanco-Fombona, *Bolívar pintado por sí mismo*. Biblioteca

Popular Venezolana, no. 67 (Caracas: Ediciones del Ministerio de Educación, 1959), p. 203.

55. SIMÓN BOLÍVAR, *Obras*, vol. I, p. 181.

56. IDALECIO LIÉVANO AGUIRRE, *Bolívar*, segunda edición (Bogotá: Editorial Liberal, n.d.), p. 185.

57. *Ibid.*, p. 187.

58. JOSÉ ANTONIO PÁEZ, *Autobiografía* (Caracas: Librería y Editorial del Maestro, 1946), vol. I, p. 215.

59. LUIS B. PRIETO F., *En esta hora* (Caracas: Federación Venezolana de Maestros, 1946), p. 70.

60. RUFINO BLANCO-FOMBONA, *Letras y letrados de Hispanoamérica* (Paris: Librería Olendorff), p. 217.

61. SIMÓN BOLÍVAR, *Obras*, vol. I, p. 1226.

62. *Ibid.*, p. 590.

63. In a letter to Robert Wilson, Bolívar said, "Bad laws and a dishonest administration have broken the Republic; it was ruined by the war. Corruption came after that to poison it to the very marrow and to rob us even of the hope of improving." Simón Bolívar, *Obras*, vol. II, p. 105.

64. Quoted by J. L. Salcedo Bastardo, *Visión y revisión de Bolívar* (Buenos Aires: Imprenta López, 1957), p. 212.

65. SIMÓN BOLÍVAR, "Message to the Sovereign Congress of Peru," February 10, 1825, in *Obras*, vol. II, pp. 1205–6.

66. See Rufino Blanco-Fombona, *Bolívar pintado por sí mismo*, p. 135.

67. SIMÓN BOLÍVAR, in a letter to Dr. J. Hipólito Unanue, president of the Council of Government of Peru, in *Obras*, vol. I, pp. 1140–42.

68. Quoted by Rufino Blanco-Fombona, *op. cit.*, pp. 130–31.

69. SIMÓN BOLÍVAR, *Obras*, vol. I, p. 886.

70. *Ibid.*, p. 1052.

71. *Ibid.*, p. 1073.

72. SIMÓN BOLÍVAR, "Proyecto de Constitución presentado al Congreso de Angostura en 1819: Cámara de Educación," artículo 7. In *El pensamiento constitucional hispanoamericano hasta 1830*, published on the hundred fiftieth anniversary of Venezuelan independence (Caracas: Biblioteca de la Academia de la Historia, 1961), vol. V, p. 229.

73. JEAN JACQUES ROUSSEAU, *Discours sur l'économie politique*, in *Oeuvres complets*, nouvelle édition (Paris: 1790), vol. VII, p. 300.

74. JEAN JACQUES ROUSSEAU, *Considération sur le gouvernement du Pologne*, in *Oeuvres complets*, vol. VIII, pp. 296–97.

75. JEAN JACQUES ROUSSEAU, *Emilio,* in *Obras escogidas* (Buenos Aires: Librería El Ateneo, 1950), p. 44.

76. C. HIPPEAU (editor), *L'Instruction publique en France pendant la révolution: Debats législatifs* (Paris: Librairie Académique, Didier et Cie., 1883).

77. SIMÓN BOLÍVAR, *Obras,* vol. II, p. 1294.

78. The sixteenth-century Spanish philosopher Juan Luis Vives refers to the ideas of Quintilian in his harsh criticisms of the practice of education in the household, where the payment to the tutor debases the process of instruction. Vives concludes with a proposed remedy: "A center of learning should be established in every city. Preceptors, men of proven capacity, of honor, and of conspicuous prudence, should be appointed to them. A salary from public funds should be assigned to these men. Children and young men will learn from them those arts in which they are able to be trained, taking into account their age and their natural dispositions." Juan Luis Vives, *De las disciplinas,* in *Obras completas* (Madrid: Aguilar, 1948), vol. II, p. 562.

79. SIMÓN BOLÍVAR, *Obras,* vol. II, p. 1135. La Chalotais had said, "Ignorance serves for nothing and damages everybody. It is impossible that any light should break through the darkness, and nobody can walk in darkness without getting lost." And further on he added, "Leave a man without culture, ignorant, and therefore insensible to his responsibilities, and he will become cowardly, superstitious, and perhaps cruel. If he is not taught the good, he will necessarily accommodate himself to evil. The mind and the heart cannot remain empty." Louis René de Caradeuc de la Chalotais, *Essai d'éducation national ou plan d'études pour le Jeunesse,* nouvelle édition (Paris: Chez Raynal, Libraire, 1825), pp. 3, 4. The first edition of this work dates from 1763; it was very successful and was translated into several languages.

80. DENIS DIDEROT, DEUVRES (Paris: Chez J. L. Briere, Libraire, 1821), vol. II, p. 156. Guizot, who was an outstanding figure of the restoration of the monarchy in France, stated, "When the multitude is least instructed, that is when error and seduction have the most power over it." François Guizot, *Essai sur l'histoire et sur l'état actuel de l'instruction publique en France* (Paris: Chez Maradan, Libraire, 1816), p. 5.

81. RUFINO BLANCO-FOMBONA, *El pensamiento vivo de Bolívar,* p. 42.

82. SIMÓN BOLÍVAR, *Obras,* vol. II, p. 1135.

83. *Loc. cit.*

84. Speaking of his own education in a letter to Santander, Bolívar said, ". . . it could be that Mr. de Mollien has not studied as

much as I have [in the works of] Locke, Condillac, Buffon, D'Alembert, Helvetius, Montesquieu, Mably, Filangieri, Lalande, Rousseau, Voltaire, Rollin, Berthot, and all the classics of antiquity, whether philosophers, historians, orators, or poets, and all the modern classics of Spain, France, Italy, and a good part of the English." Simón Bolívar, *Obras*, vol. I, p. 1099.

85. CHARLES DE SECONDAT, BARON DE MONTESQUIEU, *El espíritu de las leyes* (Buenos Aires: Ediciones Libertad, 1944), p. 56.

86. SIMÓN BOLÍVAR, *Obras*, vol. II, p. 1149. In the notable speech by the deputy Robaut Saint-Etienne, delivered in the National Assembly of France on December 21, 1792, as well as in others that stress the importance of enlightenment and of education, ideas are to be found similar to those expressed by Bolívar, although with a different emphasis and out of circumstances that were also different. In Robaut Saint-Etienne's speech, one reads, "The need for a sound theory of education is based on these truths: that it is enlightenment that has made the revolution and broken the chains of slavery; that man is susceptible of indefinite perfection; that this perfection depends on the enlightenment he acquires; that the more enlightened men are, the better their government has to be; that the greater their range of knowledge, the more they are aware of the value of liberty and the better they know how to preserve it; that the more fully enlightenment is found to be within the reach of all, the greater will be the equality maintained among men." *L'Instruction publique en France pendant la révolution: Débats législatifs.*

87. SIMÓN BOLÍVAR, *Obras*, vol. II, p. 1136.

88. *Ibid.*, p. 16.

89. CLAUDE ADRIEN HELVÉTIUS, *De l'Homme*, in *Oeuvres complets*, (Paris: Chez Seviere, Libraire, 1795), vol. IV, pp. 333 ff.

90. JUAN AMÓS COMENIO (in English, John Amos Comenius), *Didáctica magna* (Madrid: Editorial Reus, 1922), p. 61.

91. SIMÓN BOLÍVAR, *op. cit.*, vol. II, pp. 1290–91.

92. *Ibid.*, vol. I, p. 1073.

93. SIMÓN BOLÍVAR, "Carta de Jamaica," *ibid.*, p. 160.

94. RUFINO BLANCO-FOMBONA, *El pensamiento vivo de Bolívar*, p. 18.

95. SIMÓN BOLÍVAR, *Obras*, vol. II, p. 1149.

96. *Ibid.*, p. 1151.

97. *Ibid.*, p. 1150.

98. *Ibid.*, pp. 1132 ff.

99. *Ibid.*, vol. I, p. 166.

100. *Ibid.*, p. 1279.

101. Simón Bolívar, as quoted by Rufino Blanco-Fombona, *El pensamiento vivo de Bolívar*, p. 58.

102. Rufino Blanco-Fombona, *op. cit.*, p. 21.

103. Simón Bolívar, *Obras*, vol. I, pp. 442, 443.

104. *Ibid.*, p. 963.

105. *Ibid.*, p. 164.

106. Simón Bolívar, "Discurso ante el Congreso de Angostura," *Obras*, vol. II, p. 1143.

107. Simón Bolívar, *Obras*, vol. II, p. 1150.

108. Mirkine Guetzevitch, *Las nuevas constituciónes del mundo* (Madrid: Editorial España, 1931).

109. Simón Bolívar, "Proyecto de Constitución presentado al Congreso de Angostura en 1819: El Poder Moral," sección II, artículo 4. *El pensamiento constitucional hispanoamericano hasta 1830*, vol. V, p. 226.

110. In the Virginia Bill of Rights, one reads, "3. That government is, or ought to be, instituted for the common benefit, protection, and security of the people, nation, or community; of all the various modes and forms of government, that is best which is capable of producing the greatest degree of happiness and safety, and which is most effectually secured against the danger of maladministration; and that when any government shall be found inadequate or contrary to these purposes, a majority of the community hath an indubitable, inalienable, and indefeasible right to reform, alter, or to abolish it, in such manner as shall be judged most conducive to the public weal."

111. *El pensamiento constitucional hispanoamericano hasta 1830*, vol. V, p. 89.

112. Constitución de 1819, sección II, Deberes del ciudadano: *op. cit.*, vol. V, p. 186.

113. Constitución de 1819, título V, Del Soberano y del Ejercicio de la Soberanía, artículo 2: *op. cit.*

114. In a letter dated May 26, 1826, from Lima, the Liberator said, upon sending the proposed Constitution of Bolivia to General José Antonio Páez, "All the four great guarantees are preserved [in the proposed constitution]: liberty, equality, security, and property. Federal principles have been adopted to a certain point, and that of monarchical government will be satisfied too. This constitution is a middle term between federalism and monarchy." Simón Bolívar, *Obras*, vol. I, p. 1340. This acknowledgment, which tends in part to gratify the monarchical sentiments of Páez, who had asked the Liberator to take on the imperial crown, confirms the thesis I have been sustaining here. When

the government had been designed as a great centralizing power, Bolívar resorted to the establishment of the censors in order to alleviate its dominating powers.

115. "The right of resistance to oppression," says Sánchez Viamonte, "turns out to be naturally excluded by constitutionalism and, in a very special way—by the existence of a *juridical* power, acknowledged as the administrator of justice, when it is invested with the characteristics of *judicial* power, that is, of a *public* power on an equal level in the institutional hierarchy with the other two powers of the government; and thus, any oppressive wrong, even if it originates in ordinary law, can be neutralized and its faults corrected by means of judicial decision." Carlos Sánchez Viamonte, *Manual de derecho político* (Buenos Aires: Editorial Biblioteca Argentina, 1959), pp. 164–65.

116. SIMÓN BOLÍVAR, "Discurso de presentación del proyecto constitucional de Bolivia," in *Suplemento de las obras completas del Libertador,* no. 41 (Caracas: Imprenta de la Oficina Técnica del Ministerio de Defensa, July 1952), p. 9.

117. "Since the Senate watches over the public," said Montesquieu, "it is appropriate that the public, by means of its censors, keep the Senate under surveillance. It is necessary for the censors to re-establish in the republic everything that has fallen into decay, that they reprehend indifference, judge negligence, correct mistakes, just as the laws punish all crimes." Farther on, Montesquieu, in order to justify the existence of censors in a republic, says, "In what kind of government are the censors necessary? In the republic, because the fundamental principle of this kind of government is virtue. And virtue is destroyed not only by crimes, but by carelessness, by negligence, by mistakes, by apathy in love of country, by bad examples, by seeds of corruption; no longer only that which is illegal, but all that which, without being against the law, eludes it, not that which destroys the law, but all that which weakens the law or that annuls the law by letting it be forgotten—all this should be corrected by the censors." Charles de Secondat, Baron de Montesquieu, *El espíritu de las leyes,* pp. 67, 84.

118. J. L. SALCEDO BASTARDO, *Visión y revisión de Bolívar,* p. 242.

119. MANUEL FRAGA IRIBARNE, "La evolución de las ideas de Bolívar sobre los poderes del Estado y sus relaciones," *Revista de estudios políticos* (Madrid), nos. 117–18 (May and August 1961).

120. JEAN JACQUES ROUSSEAU, *Considération sur le gouvernement de Pologne,* in *Oeuvres complets,* vol. VIII.

121. ANNE ROBERT JACQUES TURGOT, quoted by Lorenzo Luzuriaga, *Historia de la educación pública* (Buenos Aires: Losada, 1946), pp. 62–63.

122. JACQUES HENRI BERNARDIN DE SAINT-PIERRE, quoted by Lorenzo Luzuriaga, *op. cit.*, p. 66.

123. MARIE JEAN DE CARITAT, MARQUIS DE CONDORCET, *Rapport et Projet de Décret sur l'organisation générale de l'instruction publique*, presentes à l'Assemblée Nationale, au nom du Comité d'Instruction Publique, par M. Condorcet, Député du Department de Paris, les 20 et 21 de avril 1792 (Paris: Imprimés par ordre de l'Assemblée Nationale, 1792), p. 5.

124. *Ibid.*, pp. 3–4.

125. SIMÓN BOLÍVAR, "Proyecto de Constitución presentado al Congreso de Angostura en 1819: Poder Moral," sección 3, artículo 2, in *El pensamiento constitucional hispanoamericano hasta 1830*, vol. V.

126. The French educational psychologist Maurice Debesse calls "age of the nursery" the period extending from the day of birth to the age of three. Debesse says, "The stage that extends from birth to the age of three is really a period of care. Education during this time is child culture, and in that moment it recovers its old sense of nutrition. To educate a baby is, in truth, to feed its body and its necessities carefully, for they are increasing incessantly. That implies concerns whose detail might seem insipid to some, but which, on the contrary, are worthy of the full attention of the educator. In fact, at this moment, the fate of the child has its beginning, although it is not yet put into play." Maurice Debesse, *Las estapas de la educación* (Buenos Aires: Editorial Nova, 1955).

127. JUAN AMÓS COMENIUS, *Didáctica magna*, p. 268.

128. SIMÓN BOLÍVAR, "Apéndice de la Constitución de Angostura," sección 3, artículo 10, in *El pensamiento constitucional hispanoamericano hasta 1830*, vol. V, p. 230.

129. See the text of these decrees, the first in *Revista de la Sociedad Bolivariana de Venezuela*, vol. XXII, no. 77 (December 17, 1963), p. 879; the second in *Codificación Nacional de Colombia*, vol. IV, pp. 103 ff.

130. JEAN JACQUES ROUSSEAU, *Emilio* (Libro III), in *Obras escogidas*, pp. 233, 258–59.

131. Comenius, in spite of his idea that people ought to be taught to be wise through the study of the sky and the earth, of beeches and oaks, that is, by investigating things for themselves and not by means of observations made by others, did come out in favor

of the utilization of textbooks. To that end he wrote, among other manuals, the *Orbispictus,* a kind of universal illustrated encyclopedia. Said Comenius, "We must choose basic books in the arts and in languages, or see that they are written, small in size but remarkable in usefulness, which explain the subjects concisely, offering much in a few words." Juan Amós Comenius, *Páginas escogidas,* con una introducción de Jean Piaget (Havana: University of Havana). Diderot too had said, in his plan for the Russian University sent to Catherine II, "It is also desirable that they have catechisms of ethics and of politics, that is, primers in which the elementary notions of national laws, of the duties of the citizens, are to be given for the instruction and use of the people, and a kind of ordinary catechism, in which a clear and simple idea of the most common things of civil life is given, as well as of weights and measures, different social conditions and professions, and of all those things that it is proper for even the least of the citizens to know." Denis Diderot, *Oeuvres,* vol. II.

132. *L'Instruction publique en France pendant la révolution: Débats législatifs.*

133. MARIE JEAN DE CARITAT, MARQUIS DE CONDORCET, *Rapport et Projet de Décret sur l'organisation générale de l'instruction publique,* title II, article 1, paragraphs V, VIII.

134. Venezuelan Decree No. 567 of the President of the Republic, promulgated in June 1966, might be thought of as a distant reverberation of the ideas of the Liberator concerning the Commission on Education, since, in a satisfactory way and paying attention to the requirements of the times, it orders the preparation of textbooks for primary schools by technical commissions in accordance with present scientific standards.

135. SIMÓN BOLÍVAR, "Apéndice de la Constitución de Angostura," sección 3, artículo 7, in *El pensamiento constitucional hispanoamericano hasta 1830,* vol. V, pp. 230–31.

136. SIMÓN BOLÍVAR, "Discurso ante el Congreso de Angostura," in *Obras,* vol. II, p. 1149.

137. SIMÓN BOLÍVAR, "Apéndice de la Constitución de Angostura," sección 3, artículos 8 y 9, in *El pensamiento constitucional hispanoamericano hasta 1830,* vol. V, p. 230.

138. JUAN AMÓS COMENIUS, *Páginas escogidas,* p. 150.

139. JUAN LUIS VIVES, *Obras completas,* vol. II, pp. 550–51.

140. SIMÓN BOLÍVAR, "Apéndice de la Constitución de Angostura," sección 3, artículo 12, *ibid.,* p. 231.

141. QUINTILIAN, *Instituciones oratorias* (Buenos Aires: Joaquín Gil, 1944), p. 46.

142. JUAN LUIS VIVES, *Obras completas*, vol. II, p. 156.

143. JUAN AMÓS COMENIUS, *Páginas escogidas*, p. 191.

144. DENIS DIDEROT, *Oeuvres*, vol. II.

145. JEAN JACQUES ROUSSEAU, *Emilio*, in *Obras escogidas*, pp. 280–81.

146. DENIS DIDEROT, *Oeuvres*, vol. II, p. 162.

147. SIMÓN BOLÍVAR, *Obras*, vol. II, p. 1296.

148. DENIS DIDEROT, *Oeuvres*, vol. II, p. 225. François Guizot, who published Diderot's work on the Russian University in *Annales de l'Education* in 1813, noted that "this idea was very popular in Diderot's times. It is impossible for us to conceive of a reasonable way of applying it." This opinion of Guizot's is inserted as a note in the second volume of Diderot's *Oeuvres*.

149. LOUIS RENÉ DE CARADEUC DE LA CHALOTAIS, *Essai d'éducation nationale*, pp. 85–86.

150. SIMÓN BOLÍVAR, *Obras*, vol. II, p. 1295. The Austrian psychologist F. Oliver Brachfeld published an article entitled "Bolívar, pedagogo moderno" in the *Revista de la Sociedad Bolivariana de Venezuela*, vol. XI, no. 31 (July 24, 1951). The author refers to the Liberator's ideas on the teaching of history, but seems to be completely unaware of these antecedents. In fact, he says, "This idea [of the retrospective method in teaching history] is all the more surprising to me on account of my having been one who has always recommended a complete change in the teaching of history, unfortunately without having had any reverberations in contemporary pedagogy." *Ibid.*

151. JEAN JACQUES ROUSSEAU, *Emilio*, in *Obras escogidas*, p. 336.

152. *Ibid.*, p. 339.

153. MANUEL B. COSSÍO, *De su jornada: Fragmentos* (Madrid: 1929), pp. 27–28.

154. SIMÓN BOLÍVAR, *Obras*, vol. II, p. 1295.

155. DENIS DIDEROT, *Oeuvres*, vol. II, p. 192. In confirmation of these opinions about mathematics, the judgment of a man of our own times, José Ortega y Gasset, might be cited. Ortega observes, "Mathematics, although very extensive, is after all counted beans. If today it seems so difficult, this is because labor is not being expended directly on the task of simplifying the teaching of it." José Ortega y Gasset, *El libro de las misiones* (Buenos Aires: Espasa-Calpe Argentina, 1945). A strong reaction against the traditional teaching of mathematics, as a skull cracker imposed on the young, is in progress, and at present a system of

methods is being experimented with under the name of "new mathematics."

156. Simón Bolívar, *Obras,* vol. II, pp. 1295–96.

157. *Ibid.,* p. 1296.

158. Diderot, *Oeuvres,* vol. II.

159. Platón, *La República* (Madrid: Librería de Perlado, Pérez y Cía., 1923).

160. Quintilian, *Instituciones oratorias,* pp. 69–70.

161. John Locke, *Pensamientos acerca de la educación,* traducción y notas de Domingo Barnés (Madrid: Ediciones de la Lectura), p. 245.

162. John Locke, *Ensayos,* as quoted in Gabriel Compayre.

163. Jean Jacques Rousseau, *Emilio,* in *Obras escogidas,* p. 201.

164. Simón Bolívar, *Obras,* vol. II, p. 1296.

165. Jean Jacques Rousseau, *ibid.,* pp. 276–77.

166. *Ibid.,* from pp. 275–86.

167. John Locke, *Pensamientos acerca de la educación,* p. 274.

168. Simón Bolívar, *Obras,* vol. II, p. 1296.

169. Quintilian, *Instituciones oratorias,* pp. 526, 532.

170. Jean Jacques Rousseau, *ibid.,* p. 152. Already at the end of the sixteenth century, in his elegant style, Montaigne asked that the tutor who is to teach should be chosen "with the head well informed, rather than well furnished and full." He spoke against the uselessness of retaining rules in the memory, and proposed as a better procedure "impregnating the child's own disposition with them." Because, according to Montaigne, "to know by memory is not to know; it is to preserve what has been deposited in the memory. When we really know something, we are able to do with it as we please, without looking at the model and without turning our eyes furtively toward some book." Michel de Montaigne, *Ensayos pedagógicos,* traducción y prólogo de Luis de Zuleta (Madrid: Ediciones de la Lectura, 1925), pp. 73, 77. Locke too spoke against excesses in the use of the memory. "When a man's head is stuffed," he said, "you have everything needed to make a pedant out of him, and this is the best way of becoming one." He spoke against an immoderate training and stated that "the things that our spirit applies its attention to, and that excite our interest, are those that one best remembers." John Locke, *Pensamientos acerca de la educación,* pp. 239–41.

171. Jean Jacques Rousseau, *ibid.,* pp. 144, 145.

172. *Ibid.,* pp. 151, 152.

173. L. Perú de Lacroix, *Diario de Bucaramanga,* p. 337.

174. Simón Bolívar, *Obras,* vol. II, p. 1296.

175. ALFRED BINET, *Ideas modernas acerca de los niños* (Madrid: 1910). At a distance of about four centuries, Binet agrees with the statements of Juan Luis Vives, who said, "Even during the first years, you ought to exercise the memory, which grows in rhythm with that exercise. Entrust to its accuracy many and frequent commissions, since at that age the child does not feel the effort, because it does not suffer wear and tear. In this way, without work and without anxiety, the memory is enlarged and comes to have an astounding capacity." Juan Luis Vives, *Obras completas*, vol. II, p. 583. As is obvious, Vives agrees with Quintilian on the matter of the development of the memory through exercise but differs from him about the fatigability of the memory by being overburdened.

176. WILLIAM STERN, *Psicología general* (Buenos Aires: Editorial Paidos, 1951), vol. I, p. 421.

177. SIMÓN BOLÍVAR, *Obras*, vol. II, p. 1294.

178. QUINTILIAN, *Instituciones oratorias*, p. 38.

179. JEAN JACQUES ROUSSEAU, *Emilio*, in *Obras escogidas*, p. 159.

180. We refer again to the article entitled "Bolívar, pedagogo moderno," in which, with observable exaggeration, Brachfeld states that "Bolívar truly becomes the precursor—almost the only one in the whole history of culture—of what at present bears the name, in the teaching of reading, of 'the global method.'" At least he corrects this statement later on and says, "We cannot pretend that Bolívar actually did proclaim the 'global method'; the procedure he recommends seems rather to occupy a middle place between ancient and modern practices." F. Oliver Brachfeld, "Bolívar, pedagogo moderno," *Revista de la Sociedad Bolivariana de Venezuela*, vol. XI, no. 31 (July 24, 1951). However, the method proposed by Bolívar was a synthetic one, differing from the global method, which is analytical since it sets out from the phrase or the word, while what the Liberator proposed was "to make children very skillful in the knowledge of the letters, and afterward in the pronunciation of the syllables." Simón Bolívar, *Obras*, vol. II, p. 1294. Once this domination over the elements has been achieved, the synthetic process in reading can be initiated.

181. Locke had previously placed great emphasis on the study of civil law. In fact, he pointed out, "When the child has sufficiently studied Cicero's *Duties* and has united that study with the Pufendorf's *De officio hominis et civis*, it will be time to let him know Grotius's *De jure belli et pacis*, or something that is worth more than the two together, Pufendorf's full treatise.

De jure naturae et gentium—here he will learn the natural rights of man, the origin and function of the state, and the duties that result from them. These general questions of civil law and of history are studies that a gentleman must not limit himself to studying superficially; it is necessary that he occupy himself with them without ceasing, that he never cease studying them." John Locke, *Pensamientos acerca de la educación*, p. 250.

182. SIMÓN BOLÍVAR, in *El pensamiento constitucional hispanoamericano hasta 1830*, vol. V, p. 230.

183. LOUIS RENÉ DE CARADEUC DE LA CHALOTAIS, *Essai d'éducation nationale*, p. 33.

184. GEORG KERSCHESTEINER, *El alma del educador: El problema de la formación del maestro*, segunda edición (Barcelona: Editorial Labor, 1934), p. 37.

185. JEAN JACQUES ROUSSEAU, *Considération sur le gouvernement de Pologne*, in *Oeuvres complets*, vol. VIII.

186. In another part of his book Kerschesteiner says, "It is not pedagogical knowledge, nor is it great erudition that makes the educator." Georg Kerschesteiner, *op. cit.*, p. 39. Pestalozzi, who was a contemporary of Bolívar, is thought of as the ideal type of teacher. He confessed to Karl Ritter, "I do not know how to count, nor how to write, nor do I understand grammar, mathematics, or anything about science. I am nothing but the one who has awakened the institution, while others must carry out in detail what I have thought. I am quite simply an instrument in the hands of Providence." Johann Heinrich Pestalozzi, as quoted by Georg Kerschesteiner, *op. cit.*, p. 39.

187. *L'Instruction publique en France pendant la révolution, Débats législatifs.*

188. JUAN AMÓS COMENIO, *Páginas escogidas*, p. 145.

189. JOHN LOCKE, *Pensamientos acerca de la educación*, pp. 56–57.

190. *Ibid.*, pp. 55–58.

191. SIMÓN BOLÍVAR, *Obras*, vol. II, p. 1292.

192. JOHN LOCKE, *op. cit.*, pp. 96–97, 108–9.

193. SIMÓN BOLÍVAR, *Obras*, vol. II, p. 1295.

194. JUAN AMÓS COMENIO, *Páginas escogidas*, pp. 79–80.

195. JOHN LOCKE, *op. cit.*, sections V, VI, pp. 69–80.

196. SIMÓN BOLÍVAR, *Obras*, vol. II, p. 371.

197. *Ibid.*, vol. I, p. 44.

198. JULES MANCINI, *Bolívar y la emancipación de las colonias españolas*, pp. 485–86.

199. *Ibid.*, p. 470.

200. JUAN AMÓS COMENIO, *Didáctica magna*, p. 203.

201. Prior to Comenius and Rousseau, Juan Luis Vives said, "The things that you see being criticized or corrected, not only in yourself but in others as well, causes them not to be lost from your memory, sometimes because you do not need to be corrected twice for the same error, at other times because seeing others being corrected is translated into benefits for yourself, since the wise man takes warning in this life from the errors of others." Juan Luis Vives, *Obras completas,* vol. II, p. 329.

202. SIMÓN BOLÍVAR, *Obras,* vol. I, p. 1342.

203. GERHARD MASUR, *Simón Bolívar,* primera edición española (Mexico: Biografías Gandesa, 1960), p. 165.